Hands

Lauren Brown

Hands

**An anxious
mind
unpicked**

Harper
North

HarperNorth
Windmill Green
Mount Street
Manchester M2 3NX

A division of
HarperCollins*Publishers*
1 London Bridge Street
London SE1 9GF

www.harpercollins.co.uk

HarperCollins*Publishers*
Macken House, 39/40 Mayor Street Upper
Dublin 1, D01 C9W8, Ireland

First published in hardback by HarperNorth in 2022
This paperback edition published 2023

1 3 5 7 9 10 8 6 4 2

Every effort has been made to contact copyright owners

A catalogue record for this book
is available from the British Library

ISBN 978-0-00-846579-7

Printed and bound in the UK using 100%
renewable electricity at CPI Group (UK) Ltd

For Liv

Contents

Prologue

I didn't give my hands much thought before they turned against me. They've not attempted to snatch away my life in any literal sense – thankfully my unwell brain and its troubled, dexterous agents have never veered in that direction – but at the time I'm, we're, writing this, it would not be untrue to say that they have been chipping away at my life, slowly, slowly, in a way I could never have predicted.

For as long as I can remember my energy has, like wild electricity, pooled in my fingertips, as though I'd be able at any moment to shoot out lightning bolts. But that's been the problem: my inability to shoot out lightning bolts. The energy has to go somewhere, do something, and I've found the solution sadly isn't as easy or as cool as that. There's no grand peroration, no ecstatic relief from anxiety, no clean-cut explanation why for me it pools in hands that are constantly, though I hope not irreparably, in motion.

I hope that by tracing my many foiled attempts to expel the tension forever expanding in me, filling me up and up until I feel I might burst, my hands and I might be able to start again. Turn over a new leaf. After all, they stroke my beautiful dog Zelda, run through my partner's hair like water, bring delicious food to my lips, give comfort as well as pain. They're helping me write this, sat on my sofa listening to a playlist called Indie Folk Music for Focus – which, I have to say, is doing the opposite job as I simply can't understand why creator Julien Delenclos wouldn't call it Folkus; if you're reading this, Julien, I want answers.

We need to get on better terms, my hands and I. They're probably tired too; we all of us need peace. So maybe I don't need lightning bolts. Maybe, like the punch of a typewriter, sporadic at first and then rhythmic, flowing, maybe whatever foreign presence is unsettling us can leave us slowly as I write. Perhaps I can get it – whatever *it* is – out. Maybe by the time I've expelled it – which I hope these strings of words can be, an expulsion – I'll softly close the lid of my laptop and feel able to sit with my hands on my lap, still. Maybe by sitting in its acquaintance, getting to know it, we won't want to expel it at all. Or maybe my heart and mind and hands will be off again like a hurricane.

The difference even then, though, would be that we will know we have turned nothing into something. That we didn't destroy but created.

But hold your horses, some subterranean voice rasps. What if there's no *it* to expel; what if it's just … you? Me. Us. This is my least favourite theory and I try not to think about it too much. It turns out I have, over the past couple of years, been trying to avoid my chaotic maelstrom of thoughts, each rushing by like a high-speed train, by drowning them out altogether. This tactic has been as horrendously ill-advised as you might expect. I've discovered the hard way that thoughts always manage to find their way out. More on this later, but for now suffice to say it's easier to shut a tangled mess of wires away in a drawer than to sit and patiently tease out the phone charger you actually need. I just don't have any patience, not when all of time is condensed into a too-bright present threatening my senses and pounding my heart. In many ways, this is an exercise in expanding time. Sitting in it. My fingers are already rapidly bashing the keys, getting it out. *Get out*.

I figured it was too dangerous to step out in front of the train; it's just common sense. I travelled from Darlington to Cambridge via Peterborough often when I was studying in Cambridge, and I'd always lose my breath when a high-speed train rushed through Peterborough, not stopping there, threatening to suck me (back pressed against the window of the Pumpkin Cafe) under its belly, away. No matter how far away you are from the platform edge, you can't avoid the way it breaks the wind in twain, the ruthless way it empties lungs.

I tried the Headspace app once and the silky voice encouraged me to imagine my thoughts passing me by. I remember a graphic of a little person sitting on a seat by a main road, just allowing her thoughts to drive by like crudely drawn cars, watching them without engaging. For me, though, it's always felt like that high-speed train. Like

I'm standing tiptoe in front of the line on the station plat-form, constantly on the brink of being destroyed. I try to disengage, to acknowledge that 'my thoughts aren't me' and that 'thoughts aren't necessarily true', but it's easier said than done when, well, your thoughts are you. Me. A bundle of unthinkable thoughts. A train.

Mam used to be quite into interpreting dreams when my twin sister Liv and I were little. There was a time when there would be dream encyclopaedias, palm-reading manuals and horoscopes scattered around the house, ready for consultation. According to journeyintodreams.com – a website that, with all due respect, holds no candle to the glossy nineties manual exuding platitudinous wisdom in pastel colours and textbook fonts that we would flick through – a dream about trains signifies:

- Your Path and Journey in Life
- Power and Strength
- Connection
- Stability and Structure
- Setting and Reaching Goals
- Purpose and Mission
- Movement and Motion
- New Opportunities
- Regrets and Failure

Vague and irresistible. But I've never dreamt of trains. Similar amorphous themes appear, though, in almost all the random searches I've done. According to this particular website, dreams about puppies, for example, are about *loyalty and trust, defence and protection, service and duty* – the list goes on.

Once Mam saw, or thought she saw, a black and white puppy on our front square of grass early one dewy morning, just sitting there with its tiny head cocked to one side in apparent curiosity. Even on the most usual of days this would've been a very strange occurrence in our little cul-de-sac in Billingham – a small, industrial, north-eastern town neighbouring Middlesbrough – or any cul-de-sac most likely, but today was especially auspicious (or ominous, depending on how you looked at it). That's because the previous night she'd vividly dreamt that our next-door neighbour's recently deceased father told her that they, the neighbours, should get his grandson a dog for companionship.

Whether the dog had been a real-life physical presence, looking into our living room window before darting off around the corner never to be seen again, or whether the icy clarity of the dream had slipped seamlessly into daylight as Mam sipped her instant coffee, the dog was rescued and a companion it made. Mam had a tendency, too, arising from a long and immensely difficult-to-grapple-with depression, to see and/or hear things that weren't really there. Maybe that was it.

The dining room was purple. Beneath a chandelier dripping plastic raindrops, Mam would sit at the square dining table with us, one of our palms cradled in hers. She'd explain to us, running her index finger down the young map of grooves, about what she called the lifeline (or, because it was the most important one to my mind, what I thought of as the root line), the LOVE LINE, THE CREATIVITY LINE. The crease down the edge of our pinkies revealed how many babies we would have. It could be a morbid business, with hairline fractures splintering from the root line suggesting a life cut short, or illness, but we always kept it light. Sadly, my hands kept some secrets to themselves.

We only ever ate dinner or tea at the table on birthdays or at Christmas, when Mam would make little finger sandwiches, elegantly prop up specially bought napkins in plastic flutes, and bring out scones – and Bucks Fizz or Babycham, if we were lucky.

Our Grandma, my mam's mam, would comb our hair for nits at that table, smoothing the serum down after dragging it across our scalp with that unforgiving metal comb, trying to be gentle as we wriggled impatiently. In delighted horror I once watched as she retrieved a meaty brown bug from one of our heads and cracked it between the hard nails of her thumb and forefinger. Her cheeky, deliciously dark sense of humour runs through our family, or so I see it, like a protective spell. If you don't laugh, after all, you'll cry. On a walk one time through the local ecology park – which us kids grew fearful of in time as stories circulated of walkers stumbling upon bodies hanging from trees – she grabbed a metal fence separating the muddy walkway from a field and pretended it electrocuted her. She stopped straight away with a laugh, and whether in tears or laughter, or both, we howled. Or stood silently, mouths agape. I can't remember. But I can still feel my paranoia occupying the shady gaps between deep-set trees, waiting for the unthinkable to come into view, and I can still hear the crack of that fat nit, feel the odd, shameful, pleasurable rush that rippled through me like a secret.

There's a name for what my hands have been doing to me, or perhaps what I've been inflicting on them: excoriation disorder, or dermatillomania. According to the NHS, it's a body-focused repetitive behaviour, for me manifesting in the roving of fingertips over flesh in search of foreign life, bumps and craters. Like a planet suddenly revealed to be home to deep-buried precious metal, greedily ransacked for shallow happiness. Even in the depths of the night they scan, and when I wake up there will be tender places where the surface has been so damaged, the same area tortured dozens of times, that dots of blood bloom through my cotton T-shirt. For whatever reason, I focus on my face and shoulders and chest. It can be anywhere, though, and for other people it's hands or legs or arms. Another expression takes the form of pulling hairs out; that version is called trichotillomania.

My dermatillomania has been spreading like wildfire lately, and I don't like to leave the house. I'm 15 again, unwilling to even go to the corner shop without wearing a full face of slap. Logically, I know that people won't notice the constellations of scabs on my cheeks with the telescopic precision I do – we're all so preoccupied with ourselves – but there's nothing at all logical about tearing at your own bleeding skin even while it's hurting, while it's begging you to stop, while *you're* begging you to stop. Inside my mind, I'm pummelling a thick glass window with balled fists, my mouth is moving silently, rapidly, tears are streaming down to my top lip, she's screaming at me to stop, but I can't hear her. I'm trying to.

The red marks are becoming deeper now after years of reopening old wounds, purpling like bruises in places. But still my fingers rage on, ravenous, burning pre-existing marks wider and faster than fire consuming paper, edges curling in. It used to only be my face and shoulders. All teenagers get spots and all teenagers pick them. But now my chest is raw and scarred, my face flaking, deep-scarred, and like a painter my eye still scouts fresh canvas.

It's estimated that between 1% and 5% of people suffer from dermatillomania, the vast majority being female. In the DSM-5, the fifth edition of the American Psychiatric Association's *Diagnostic and Statistical Manual of Mental Disorders*, which is widely used to help diagnose these kinds of disorders, skin picking disorder, also known as excoriation disorder, is currently categorized as an 'obsessive-compulsive and related disorder', seen as being similar to OCD but not the same. A cousin to OCD. Whatever the hell it is, I feel it's an addiction. These obsessive-compulsive and related disorders, including trichotillomania and body dysmorphic disorder, can be extremely debilitating for sufferers unable in many cases to stop damaging themselves – in my case, for the 'release' I get, the lightning-shooting-out-of-fingertips high.

It's not easy to admit to or talk about, and the commensurate shame, guilt and embarrassment are commonplace among sufferers. It has, though, been a recognised psychological disorder for well over 100 years; in 1875, English surgeon and dermatologist Erasmus Wilson (a distant relative? My grandad's a Wilson) coined the term 'neurotic excoriation' to describe out-of-control picking behaviours. It's not often spoken about because, well, it's embarrassing. And because they're 'normal' behaviours that have spiralled out of control, telling people often prompts a 'just stop then' response. I've been asked whether I'm self-harming ('no, or at least, I don't think I am in the way you're implying') and why I'm doing it ('I don't know, doctor, that's why I came').

It's never simple. Like all psychiatric disorders, a whole entangled world of experiences, triggers, traumas, days out at the beach, embraces, words you shouldn't have said, words you wish you had said, all of it, lies beneath. Bottled up, bubbling away beneath the surface, the resulting behaviour bursts out in weird ways that are uncomfortable to face. Such as wrecking your skin in secret.

Picture the blurred figure of a woman, sitting in a quiet room, nervously rubbing her hands together while waiting for the doctor to appear. She's hunched over, probably rehearsing in her mind the exact combination and order of words she'll use to describe what's wrong, what is to her mind the best and only way to properly communicate her ailment, though maybe that's not the right word, to a stranger. She's probably terrified of being misunderstood, diagnosed wrongly and irreversibly. Perhaps in her hands there's a crinkled note on which she's scribbled some brief prompts, things she definitely wants to mention, in case her mind goes blank, her mouth dry, breathing laboured. She's so nervous she unconsciously runs her fingers over her face, pausing at any irregularities, as she tries to compose her thoughts and slow her beating heart.

Our subject is the 47-year-old patient of William James Erasmus Wilson, the man who brought 'neurotic excoriation' into psychiatric, if not common, parlance. She was initially known to me only as *Case 1.– A maiden lady*, referenced as such in one of Wilson's Lectures on Dermatology delivered between 1871 and 1873 to England's Royal Society of Surgeons. But as I read her story, I unwittingly started calling her Lacy.

In the run-up to her appointment Lacy had been reading to a deaf person in a 'close, hot room' for five hours a day. No more information is given on this unusual titbit. Perhaps the person wasn't completely deaf, could lip-read, or maybe it was simply for companionship. Who knows? Whatever the case, the activity gave rise to a 'considerable exhaustion' apparently compounded by Lacy's anxiety to perform the duty satisfactorily. I imagine the room lined with heavy, faded, green-velvet curtains that trail the floor, thick rugs and shadows. Lacy sits on an unexceptional wooden chair, reading aloud and worrying whether she's trying hard enough to do it well.

Prologue

Although this particular iteration of her unquiet mind is relatively new, Wilson notes, she has since her twenties suffered from bouts of fainting and 'considerable strain on her nerves'. She 'has the face spotted over' with 15–20 small abrasions of various ages. A couple are fresh wounds. Others are dulling, darker – old but kept alive by her unstoppable, agitated hands.

She explains that the rise of spots and bumps is accompanied by a sense of 'fullness', itchiness and irritation, and that she has 'no chance of peace until she … rubbed them or scratched them and produced a flow of blood'. I know the feeling. Wilson eruditely observes that 'in that case, the uneasiness ceased'. But if he got close to glimpsing the truth of the disorder, he was unfortunately a bloke very much of his time, speculating that the cause of her strange malady could be 'perverted religious enthusiasm', or perhaps – you guessed it – 'sexual irritation', inadvertently hitting on the immutable fact that no one can have it all.

The more I've spoken about my disorder, the longer its tail has become and the more I've thought about Lacy. I've felt connected to her in the fear and confusion we've felt, more than a century apart, the snowball gathering pace until it floors us. The blood we've both shed, the sleepless nights.

Memories have floated to the surface unbidden. Objects, moments – sometimes whole, other times not; sometimes funny, sometimes devastating – have illuminated my lifeline, like a helicopter floodlight sweeping a star-cloaked Grand Canyon that's but a scratch on the earth's crust the further you zoom out, up, away. The thin lines that break off from the root line, which at times looks like it spirals into a DNA helix before becoming beguilingly straight again, all the mess untangles for a brief moment, and in those brief moments, I'm – me, Lauren – there.

We're typing this now, my hands and I, journeying through the canyon, poised to travel back to before the great rift started widening, deepening, in the hope that we can look not in fear but in wonder at the scar in me we caught, just in time.

1
Bird

We found the baby – 'bird' wouldn't apply for a while yet – on the cold side of our front garden on a thin slab of concrete below the living room window. It looked barely alive, so translucent you could see its insides. A withering umbilical cord hung, tiny, from its little round belly, and its eyes – impossibly large, heavily lidded in purple – hadn't opened yet. It lay on the cold, damp concrete beside the bush that separated our square of grass from next door's gravel drive. Or maybe it was across the lawn and on the public pavement where we found him (I still think of him as a him). He just lay there, barely breathing, an unbearably thin layer of bare, pink skin stopping his organs from mingling with the dirt and stone of the cold floor. Holding him together. Just.

Mam, Liv – my twin sister – and I scooped him up in a tissue. His ribs were tiny, like fish bones; you could see each one. Mam said he must've fallen from his mother's wings as she flew him to their nest. Even now, that seems unreasonable, improbable. Surely she'd have known her goo wouldn't provide adhesive enough to keep her newborn baby close. The cruel tragedy of a lack of hands, I thought, my young heart pounding with the urgency of life and death. If only she'd been able to *really* hold him. Did birds not use their beaks like cats grabbing their young, rough, by their scruffs? Maybe she had, and dropped him from her mouth. Maybe she felt him slipping and her quick mother's instinct dropped him in the shadowy corner away from predators. Thinking of her in her nest without him made me want to cry.

Every second stretched wide as I begged a God I might have still believed in to spare him, desperately wanting to feel the whisper of his heartbeat against my palms. Desperate for him to understand through the warmth and comfort of my skin that I cared. I cared so hard, in the way perhaps only a child can.

It was as though Mam had prepared her whole life for this very moment, first offering the 'stuck to the wings' theory before, without a second's thought it seemed, packing a bowl full of warm, damp kitchen roll to place him gently in. There was a flash of recognition not yet fully formed that my mother had thoughts and possibly even experiences beyond my own, beyond me: a fully-fledged self outside of the Mam I knew. Where had she acquired such knowledge? Knowledge so far away, I thought, from our experiences.

The bowl was put on top of the small fireplace. The fire had a glass pane behind which lumps of coal sat, and on which Liv and I would, when we were littler, gleefully melt multicoloured crayons. We fed our bird tiny bits of damp bread through a syringe, which we apparently had. It had probably emerged from the drawer of junk and bits next to the cutlery drawer. Then there was the awkward business of going about our daily lives: having chicken nuggets and chips in front of the telly, watching the usual string of kids, shows followed by *The Simpsons* and the soaps, while he silently battled for survival in his lonely makeshift nest. The moment of crisis inevitably softened into the flow of days and we settled into the new atmosphere of our living room, the new reality we lived in, thin as a thread. We fed him and we waited.

Eventually, his sealed, swollen eyes opened. Joy of joys, the crumbs soaked in milk and water were working. God knows what first impression lay deep within those pools of absolute black, surrounded as he was by our yellow-painted living room, yellow sofa and red cushions (that was the theme at the time; it would go through many B&Q and Boyes trips yet). We loomed over him, gawping, wanting to touch. Where were his wriggling siblings? Perhaps high up among the leaves and brushed by a cooling breeze. He likely awoke to the sound of *Dick and Dom in da Bungalow* instead of hungry chirping or the distant call of other birds caught on the coastal wind. He soon filled the room with his own voice. He warbled, shrieked, his mouth a wide open 'O' with a darting tongue raised to the air. Often.

Though we were sadly unable – or rather, unwilling – to cater to his taste for regurgitated matter, the syringe food nevertheless seemed to be doing the trick and, like any healthy young lad, no matter how much he got he cried and cried for more.

Ecstatically, we watched him change. The constellations of red and purple veins were replaced at pace with the stubble of emergent feathers, the ornithological parallel to too-big teeth protruding awkwardly from kids' shiny, pink gums. They grew like leaves from small, twisted things before emerging in patches like teenage stubble.

THEN HE CHOKED TO DEATH.

At least we think that's what happened.

We didn't hear it or realise at first. Just, I assume, found him sleeping in his bowl one day. Maybe after school. I don't remember, but I do remember Mam breaking the news that a bit of his food had, it seemed, got stuck on the way down. Maybe it was too big, I thought angrily, but he'd survived for what must've been two weeks to that point, and each day she'd given him the same amount of food. It seemed like he'd been thriving, hot life running through his veins ever more assuredly, and then he just went.

Sadness hung like a rock in a blanket in me, feeling heavier at times than others. Had it been a freak accident? Or had we unwittingly tortured a poor, helpless being for two weeks? Would he ever have survived without his mother? What had he thought, if anything? If my faith, nurtured and cultivated by a Catholic primary school, was a string tying me to a God, I'm sure it was thinning, fraying. But even so I felt watched in some damning, judgemental way.

In reception class I'd had a teacher who I simultaneously remember as being both sweet and unconscionably cruel. She'd get annoyed and shout at me whenever I needed a wee, which, either because of or in spite of the reaction I knew I'd get, would only make me need it all the more. I can still remember the smell of the child-sized bathroom that seems now like something out of *Charlie and the Chocolate Factory*, or a doll's house. Once, when I stood up, the cold black porcelain nipped my bum and I cried and cried in agony. I remember her anger. I think the impulse, which has in different ways dug its claws into me ever since, to dispel the anticipation of her wrath by, whether I needed the toilet or not (probably convincing myself I needed it, for no child could go *that* often) telling her I did, started here; the impulse to just 'get it out of the way'. I still feel profoundly anxious going anywhere I'm not in close proximity to a known public toilet. My worst nightmare is a Megabus with an out-of-order loo.

The words 'coach' and 'bus' continue to send a shiver down my spine today. We were returning home from a Year 9 trip to Lanehead in the Lake District. Liv, my friends and I had joyously rambled, gill-scrambled, and scraped our knees; we'd put our phones down and acted like the kids we were. Before we boarded – and feeling free, my anxieties and foibles cast to the north-western breeze – I did something so unlike me that to this day I can't quite believe it happened. I chugged FOUR Capri-Suns. I've endeavoured in my adult life to match this level of rock and roll ever since: to proclaim again unapologetically and unthinkingly how little I give a shit for convention, to plant a flag down hard in my freedom as if to say, chin bucked, 'Yeah, and what?' Four. Capri. Suns. You little fucking legend. But, alas, it may very well be the painful knowledge of what happened next that made me the cripplingly thoughtful adult I am today – in a 'she has so many thoughts, hope she's OK' kind of way.

Those of us who were conscientious buckled in, ready for the three or however many hours' drive. Others threw themselves into the backseats, immediately put their feet up and blasted DJ Boonie's 'Concrete Angel' out of their Sony Ericsson W850i Walkman mobiles. Whatever, let's get out of here. But not whatever. It wasn't whatever at all. The bravado in me, so bold only moments ago, crystalised into shards of panic digging at my insides, because as soon as I took my seat – somewhere between the lawlessness of the back row and the goody-two-shoesness of the front – I noticed a sign on the door I'd strategically positioned myself near. Those three, stomach-dropping words, the punch of four black syllables right to my gut, came into view: Out of Order.

You'd think I had in that moment woken up in pitch darkness buried six feet under the ground. Over the years I'd become familiar with that panic rush of coldness through the veins. One of the CBBC TV shows we watched at the time featured a young Fearne Cotton and science experiments that provoked a 'Eureka!' from giddy, wide-smiling presenters. Google's definition of the word includes this usage example: 'The answer hit me. "Eureka!" I cried.' Aptly vague, something monstrous peeking through the cracks of 'I cried'. My feeling was the ghoulish photo negative of that scene, the presenters' mouths and eyes glowing green. Eureka indeed. Eureka, I'm fucked! I cried.

I probably wasn't sitting next to Liv at this time. At that age, 13 or 14, we didn't quite appreciate or realise in any fully formed way exactly what we were to each other. If anything, we were a nuisance to one another. Or at least, I was a nuisance to Liv. That I can say with 100 per cent certainty. Around this time, we'd started staying at my dad's more often, him having come back into our lives after a few post-divorce years of inter-parental acrimony and meeting him at the end of the cul-de-sac for a hug.

MSN was our entire life. We would fight over the one laptop Dad got for us, lest we end up rocking back and forth in a corner deprived of SmarterChild (a very noughties chatbot) and boyfriends, until he eventually decided we were allowed half an hour each. The second we'd get home from school at twenty to four, the metronomic, begrudged passing of the laptop across laps would begin in frightful earnest. The atmosphere was brittle. We were the anti-Chuckle Brothers, stuck in an endless, purgatorial loop of to-me-to-you-ing. If Sisyphus had been given the option of sharing his endless uphill boulder rolling with an uphill-boulder-rolling companion, he'd say absolutely not if he had any sense. We were opposite poles of a magnet, destined to be forever together but repelled. The sun and moon, yin and yang.

This teenage angst would wear off, eventually, but here on this bus home from Lanehead it is unlikely we sat together. This distance between us was a blessing and a curse. She was the only person to whom I could disclose my sudden screaming need to go to the toilet, but I'd also have smarted painfully at the inevitable 'for God's sake' frustration that I was doing this 'again'. Now I'm older I think it's a kind of claustrophobia, and though my friends gently tease me about what is an enduring bladder-based anxiety, there's a gentle undercurrent of understanding simply unreachable by kids. In Year 4 a girl had thrust her hand desperately into the air to try and alert the teacher she needed the bathroom and was told she should've gone at lunchtime, which we all know is bullshit, and on her long grey skirt a circle of darker grey bloomed. Maybe this is what got it into my head. I don't know. But to this day I can't sit in the middle of the row at the cinema, or worse, the theatre, in case I need the toilet and have to disturb people.

The cinema has always been a bit of a trigger point for me because when I was really diddy, like even diddier than Year 4 or Dick or Dom, I'd left a screening to go for a wee on my own like a big girl, before re-entering the wrong screening and sitting down next to the wrong dad who was watching the wrong film. The first thing I'd ever seen at the pictures, *The Grinch Who Stole Christmas*, remained a mystery to me since my dad had to take me out every ten minutes. I just hate being hemmed into a confined space and the feeling that I can't get out whenever I want to without disturbing anyone and publicly humiliating myself.

So there I sat, freaking the fuck out but not saying a word to whoever I was sat next to. Considering what comes next there was probably no one sharing my seat. I was both overjoyed and devastated not to be with Liv and filled with an urgent sense that I was about to piss myself, if not filled with actual Capri-Sun piss itself (if you, dear reader, have ever had a UTI, you'll understand the impossibility of deciphering whether you're actually desperate or just *feel* desperate, a brutal severance of mind and body that would make Descartes wince). In that moment, four OJs down, there was no way of me knowing because *the fucking toilet was out of order*. Just as pain floods the mind so completely no other thoughts can squeeze in, so impossible was it for me to think of anything other than my bulging bladder and the imminent social suicide of actually wetting myself, so I probably wasn't thinking about the mind–body problem.

Eventually, after sitting squirming for what must've been a noble hour or so, I reached crisis point and, swaying, reluctantly and conspicuously walked the gangway up to the front of the bus to deliver a furtive tap on the teacher's shoulder. She was clearly agitated – she quite understandably wanted to get home after spending nine days or so in the middle of nowhere with poor phone signal and a group of thirty-odd pubescent kids – as we pulled into an abandoned-looking petrol station. The only toilet was a single stand-alone brick cubicle outside. It looked like the punishment that in my head it was. The coach devastatingly ground to a halt, just for me, and as I closed the toilet door behind me and perched my bum on the cold seat, I was overcome with utter mortification. But what bliss, what relief! It wasn't long, however, before I was struck by a grim, portentous thought. *What if I need it again? What if I have to stop the entire bus and make everyone wait for me and me alone … again?* Hello darkness, my old friend.

We were only about halfway home, I realised with a shiver, so instead of just getting back to the bus sharpish so we could hit the road again, I tried to pre-emptively squeeze out any urine I *might* need to expel further down the line. If God had presented me with an option to have one big hour-long wee in the morning instead of a rolling need depending on my liquid intake, I would've snapped his hand off. Would've enjoyed it, the big long wee, and all. No such luck. Instead, this habit would continue long after. There were spells when I'd sit on the toilet at Mam's for what seemed like hours, sure I needed a wee and forcing myself to try and go despite the fact nothing but intermittent drops were infrequently, painfully extracted. 'You don't need it, Lauren,' my Mam would say, but I was so *so* sure I did. Or might, in a bit, at least.

So I couldn't time travel. I couldn't wish future piss into my bladder, and brutal, unstoppable time had won again.

I gave up, surrendered to the vast unknowable future, and solemnly re-entered my metal prison, burdened by fate. The door pffed shut behind me in a swift motion, and I was sealed in once more. We continued our journey, and I looked pensively out of the window in a pose usually reserved for Mam's Golf on the A19 listening to 'Angels' by Robbie Williams, or Moby, palm pressed dramatically on the wind-up window as it rained.

Of course, I needed it again immediately. As the minutes slugged past, I choked back tears. Maybe if I let them fall it would cleverly lessen the need to wee? All bodily fluids came from the one in-built reservoir, no? But no, there was absolutely no way I could cry and absolutely no way I could stop the bus again. I didn't then have the language or self-knowledge to go to the teacher and explain that maybe I was claustrophobic and probably wouldn't have needed it even once had the toilet been in service. Maybe she'd have been sympathetic, but maybe she'd have been angry. I stayed quiet. The tension filling me up turned to a deep pain, and for the final two hours of the journey I prepared myself for the worst. I'd heard once that a king had died of needing the toilet, and in the back of my mind I wondered whether I too was about to meet my end.

I've always wildly catastrophised in even the most blatantly innocuous situations. When I was 15, so only a couple of years after Lanehead and this fateful coach trip, which I'll reluctantly return to in a moment, I had to go to counselling because whenever someone took a while to get back to me via text or call I'd assumed they'd died.

Like, literally shuffled off this mortal coil. A pretty distressing rigmarole to go through all day every day and a habit that took a long, long while to break. It didn't help that a boyfriend I had when I was 20 decided to text me 'Night, love you' before disappearing off the face of the earth. Suffice to say I thought he'd perished in some horrific accident, but of course I found him in his pyjamas in his shit university halls looking like he'd seen a ghost.

The less destructive flip side of this catastrophising tendency was my proclivity to be a complete and utter drama queen at every minor injury or inconvenience. Whenever I was tired as a kid I'd just cry and cry and cry. I once dropped my head asleep in a bowl of soup and I probably would've drowned had Mam not noticed. I even came out of the womb like a diva, feet first and with the cord wrapped so tightly around my neck that I was blue. Once it had been unwound and I'd been slapped on the arse like Lucien from the *Cramp Twins*' opening credits (iconic), I started crying and pretty much haven't stopped since. Liv, on the other hand, slid out like the chosen child, with a mop of black hair and huge eyes. Not a peep out of her.

She was so well behaved that when she broke her arm on a caravan holiday, aged about seven, it took five or so days of quiet whimpering, swimming trips and outdoor activities for my parents to realise. The only time an injury overwhelmed her, to my knowledge, was at a birthday party in our garden during which the neighbour brought over a life-sized inflatable Spider-Man. As he carried it under his arm past Liv, the ridge going right around the edge of it, by some terrible, terrible bad luck, scratched Liv's eyeball – her actual eyeball. I remember tears, lots of them, but I don't remember noise.

So while I was wriggling about on my ugly-patterned seat on that coach home from Lanehead, I'm sure she was colouring in or reading or else just sitting in silence with her perfectly manicured hands on her perfect lap, perfectly peaceful perfect bitch.

On that coach I knew no peace. I can honestly say those two hours were the worst of my life. At one point – and this is why it's important I was sitting on my own – I regret to say I took a couple of sanitary pads and layered them on top of each other in my knickers. I'd started my period on my grandad's birthday when I was 10 or 11 (which is a bit much), so was thankfully on this occasion stocked with what my young entrepreneurial mind suddenly saw as makeshift nappies. At a school assembly around the same time, a local entrepreneur, who I think had maybe been on *Dragons' Den*, brought in an invention to show us anything was possible and that we could be inventors too. It had been a sort of glorified pipe cleaner, bright green, with a magnet on the end for pulling wires through small holes during DIY projects. Sexy, sexy stuff. Three pads layered on top of each other was my secret contribution to the St Michael's hall of business excellence.

Once semi-successfully installed, I switched tactics from holding it in to relenting and letting it out. The desperation! But my body had other ideas. I tried with all my might to let myself just wee, but thoughts were wheeling in my head. *What if it doesn't work? You're surrounded by your classmates: what if someone sees? What if it leaks onto the floor and once you've started you can't stop?* So I didn't go. Couldn't go. After what seemed like an age, a second Dark one, we pulled up outside the school's green fence and I dashed inside to finally go. It hurt and was no relief.

This same sweet and cruel reception teacher at Our Lady of the Most Holy Rosary Catholic Primary School gave us all a lesson, once, about lying. Innocuous stuff, you'd think, to teach five-year-olds about honesty. We'd all been guilty of pretending we hadn't smashed a sandcastle in the sad plastic pit, or stolen a doll straight from someone else's grubby hands – crying snottily, confronted, as we explained they were 'hogging it'. But the hardcore Catholic bent of this class quite literally put the fear of God into me.

As we all sat slack-jawed and cross-legged in a semi-circle around her, she told us that if we told a lie (however big or small), God would give us a tummy ache and we'd feel bad. Well, I couldn't bear it. What did she mean? Would I actually vomit? *Good God*, I thought, *I'll never tell a lie again.* And for a solid couple of years, *years* as my mam tells it, I'd hastily add a 'maybe' or an 'I think so' to everything I said. Liv and I would be ready to go to sleep in our parallel single beds, our mam would shout

'Night, love you,' to which Liv would reply 'Night, love you' (like a sane person) and I'd shout 'Night, I love you, I think.' At first she'd shout back, not unkindly, 'What do you mean, you think? You daft sod,' but then it became part of the routine. Maybe as she hoovered or moved from room to room (sometimes I'd shout down to ask what room she was in, just so I knew) she'd tut or roll her eyes. *This again.*

The teacher's hellfire specificity sadly didn't extend to whether or not I'd know I was lying. What if I only realised once the belly pain started and it was too late? How could I repent if I didn't know what the lie was? How would I differentiate between a normal belly ache and a God belly ache? To my squishy mind, my only options were either to hedge my bets every time or become a frenzied bureaucrat with a car-park-sized filing system to record and rank every word that came out of my mouth. I'm not an idiot, so plumped for the former, and it worked. No belly problems, no problem. The perpetual state of fear and anxiety was apparently a small price to pay for an untroubled gut. Eventually, my mam tells me, she gently confronted me about my quirk, and with gentle coaxing I stopped saying my two favourite suffixes.

The unfilled space these words left has stayed ever since, their imprint permanent. Faced with my bird's death, my bird that wasn't ever meant to be ours, the paradoxical presence of this unfilled space – the low-level uncertainty – throbbed. Had we made him suffer?

Confined to a bowl he didn't have strength enough to leave? *Maybe*.

The field round the corner from our house is named after a college long gone. A distant memory tells me Mam went there when she was young to learn flower arranging. I can picture its buildings although I don't think I ever saw it. Maybe I saw it in a photograph once, the large square windows rounded at the corners, its sandy, reddish colour. Maybe through her eyes I'm able to see it, a genetic imprint like a faded picture. Maybe my young mind had soaked up whatever brief information she shared – 'I learnt flower arranging at the college' is quite enough to go on for a kid – and constructed it using the not-quite colours of our living room.

It wasn't there when I was young, and so the field stretched back further than it does today. Now, especially on bleak days, it looks rather sad. Nothing marks it out, there are no distinguishing features of note other than a short dip in the grass, not steep enough to be a bank. A half-feature on an otherwise plain expanse of green. There's a bland, new-looking GP surgery, but that's more to the left by John Whitehead Park.

If you walked across the field you'd get to the baked-bean-tin-shaped block of flats Dad's eccentric friend Big Michael lives in alone, right next to the town centre. Even as a little girl I thought his flat seemed like something out of a bygone age: the old fireplace, lots of brown panelling and a gramophone from the forties, a small TV and radio or record player, and sepia photographs here and there.

Big Michael was a postman, like my dad and his two brothers, but I can't believe he ever successfully finished his round. With a broad smile and in his huge, booming voice, he would stop to greet every single person. Not strangers, but local people he'd known for decades and whose family trees he'd no doubt memorised. His enthusiasm never dims. His hair has greyed but his big brown eyes swim with wonderment whenever he spots you. Through him I learnt the word 'blighter': 'you cheeky blighter', 'the old blighter'. He must have a notebook filled with birthdays, since he never misses one. When his card drops through the door, it's immediately recognisable by his almost completely illegible handwriting, though I'm something of a codebreaker now. I can't help but think of him as the Patron Saint of Billingham. These days he volunteers in the new food bank in the gloomy, orange-lit underbelly of Billingham town centre, where empty husks of shops sit. Now an abandoned lot, there used to be a butcher where Gran would get us chopped pork and Billy Bear meat slices, out of which Liv and I used to barbarically pop the eyes and mouths. There's also a gutted Silly Prices, a 'Spoons that used to be the bookshop my auntie Karen worked in, and a now-closed furniture store that sold hideous patterned sofas at Low Low Prices. The Boyes, an 80s-looking emporium of factory discards and irresistible tat, is, miraculously, still open. These are the upstairs and downstairs levels of The Dark Bit of Town.

In Boyes, you can buy comfy granny bras, tights and quality £1 eyeliner. Upstairs there are rolls and rolls of fabric and all things crafty. As a kid we'd go in after having gravy and chips at The Galley next door: a greasy spoon that had cream cakes behind glass, plastic green sofa booths, help-yourself cutlery and salt sachets, staff dressed like dinner nannies, and – crucially – coffee with condensed milk (Gran's favourite). Like everywhere else in Billingham, you'd no doubt run into someone you knew. Grandma's friend, maybe, who'd come over and tell us how she'd known us since we were 'this big' and how much we'd grown. Gran walks through the town centre like a royal, honestly, so many people does she know.

The last time I saw my uncle George – my dad's uncle – before he died unexpectedly while on holiday with his doting wife, was in The Galley. We'd never been close but you could tell his heart was enormous. Even then I marvelled at the ability of family members to love each other with the fierceness of kin and shared geographical place – a Billingham love, rooted deep – without ever really knowing each other. He wrapped us in a bear hug and we spoke, among other things, of Brexit. He was in favour, and sometimes his Facebook profile picture would have the St George's cross in it. Even as we grew up and went to uni, he'd comment on every single picture we were in: 'Love u' or 'Love u take care uncle George'. Liv confided once that she wasn't sure what to say because, not in a nasty way, she didn't love him back. Or maybe

I'm remembering wrong, and she was just uncomfortable because we hardly knew him and it was intense. In any case, I gently nudged her to just say it back – what was the harm?

In Boyes, my little hands perched on the counter with my chin on them, I'd watch huge, black-handled scissors slice through the fabric of Mam's choice. I'd try to replicate the action with paper, at school or at home, to recreate the perfect sound of the fabric being torn asunder, but I'd only get so far and the paper would rip. Also in Boyes' upstairs section were tubs and tubs of buttons of every design and colour imaginable. There were pearlescent buttons perfect for a polite cardigan, chunky plastic ones for a coat maybe, wooden ones for a more rustic look; it was miraculous.

There we'd pick up the foil scratch-art kits me and Liv used to devour as kids – you know, the ones where you'd carefully scratch away at the lines to reveal an elaborate tiger, lion, fish, or whatever. These were perfect for me, and probably the only time I displayed any modicum of patience in my life was watching the scratch-card grey peel away under my metal pen; it was so satisfying, and I was actually able to apply myself to it in earnest. A potential precursor to my picking, I was able to escape my thoughts for a while as the foil came away in perfect coils.

Beyond that, though, my attention span was (is) frazzled. Liv used to lie belly down on the living room rug and copy out the encyclopaedia, just, I suppose, for the joy of writing with a nice pen. It may seem an odd thing to do, and that's because it absolutely is, but who among us can deny the unbounded pleasure of a rollerball rolling over good paper? Mam was into calligraphy, too, so there was perhaps a desire in Liv to perfect her own handwriting. We were about the age when you'd be given your first red handwriting pen at school – a real rite of passage. She and Mam would also labour over thousand-piece jigsaws picked up from charity shops all over town. Liv coloured inside the lines, but I couldn't be arsed. What was the point? I would skip between activities – unfinished drawings, the Game Boy, the telly – like it was my last day on earth.

Mam and Dad separated when we were eight. I remember her throwing a Pot Noodle at him and it going all up the curtains. From Big Michael's flat, looking out over Billingham at the rows and rows of houses, you could see the tiny, freezing-cold house my dad lived in with his new wife, Ruth. Although it was concealed by foliage, I could also locate their neighbour's bomb shelter, right at the back of the garden.

We'd sometimes play with a girl called Billie, who was in the year below and lived a few doors down from Dad's new house. I remember standing on top of a green wheelie bin down the side of Dad's house to climb over the fence and into the neighbour's garden, rushing, crouching, to the end where we found the dusty tin shelter. Inside were what looked like two hard single beds with a sort of chest of drawers. It was dim and not much to look at, but I was completely enthralled. It was like peering through a window to another world. I'm sure if we'd just knocked and asked to have a look, the owners would have let us. But maybe Billie was worried they'd ask how she knew it was there, sheltered as it was.

I can't remember being that close to Billie, but I loved going to her house. Her dad worked for the local crisp factory (where my two cousins work now) so we'd always get BBQ crisps. They're still my favourite.

Further down the road and around the corner was a cluster of streets, like a square, where:

1. Auntie Karen lives with Dad's brother – also a postman and a former marathon runner – and their son Ben
2. Grandma and Grandad (Dad's parents) lived with the huge tree in their front garden, and
3. Uncle George had lived next to Daniel at school, on the street perpendicular.

It was like a sprawling family tree made of tarmac.

You only had to walk for about seven minutes across the field from Mam's to Dad's, they were that close, but the flat expanse of grass seemed like an ocean to lazy teenagers. It hadn't always seemed that way. Around the time the bird died, along with other local kids, we would climb a gnarled tree at the back of the field. We were a hotchpotch group, united by the streets connecting our houses, none too far away for our parents to worry. We'd all 'call for each other' to run through garden sprinklers or play kerbie.

I cannot tell you how perfect a tree for climbing it was. The branches were basically stairs, inclined at intervals just so. You could climb them like cartoon cloud steps to heaven. Not too easy, mind you. Their difficulty level was set at a cool medium to hard, meaning you would chafe your palms or a knee occasionally on the scramble up, but always with some effort get right to the top to look out over the field like the captain of a pirate ship. In my memories it's always sunny there. We'd stay until the summer night became balmy and pink and we started to get hungry. A clan thrown together by age and circumstance, that tree was absolutely everything we could ever want it to be. I remember it most as a house.

We each had our own branch, our bedroom I suppose, and we imagined each area had a different function. An upturned trolley from the Asda was our toilet. Whether we actually, you know, did the deed in there, I can't remember. I imagine we did, though, because at a school friend's house once we turned her tiny porch into a 'house' where we 'lived now' and I'm fairly sure we pissed into a bucket and chucked it out onto one of the big trees in the shared grass outside her house.

Around this time I felt the first ecstatic stirrings of young love, too. Hannah's brother, older than us by a couple of years, with the softest and brightest blond hair, joined us occasionally. When he was there it was like instead of a heart I had a summer flower blooming in my chest.

Bird

The tree was everything to us, to me. Even now I feel aglow just thinking of it. Liv and I had bikes with tassels coming out of the handlebars and we'd throw them down in the grass by the tree and scramble like the entire day didn't stretch long in front of us, like our lives depended on it.

Once, as I crossed from pavement to grass on my bike, past Hannah's house (which was round the corner from ours), the green electricity box standing on the precipice of stone and earth electrocuted me. I remember the surge through my entire arm, the force of it, and fell off my bike onto the grass. I still got to the tree, though. Maybe I was embarrassed in case her brother had seen through the window.

When the bird died, we knew we had to bury him there, the most joyous place on earth. We packed him into another tissue bed, but this time it didn't matter if it was damp or warm or felt like a nest, and instead of a bowl it was a shoebox. He was still so tiny and fragile, as still as the day we'd found him.

If I'd experienced the ritual of death before this point it can only have been of our goldfish. We had two. One was your average goldie, but another was black with eyes that popped out of its head. I think it replaced one that died, but I don't know. In any case, when we found them floating atop their bowl we wrapped them in tissue and buried them in The Dump at the bottom of Mam's garden. Flushing them down the toilet was just not an option. I no doubt worried that a fish would somehow come back up the system while my private parts were exposed to the bowl and I'd look down and it'd be there, back for revenge. I think I'd seen too many horror films too young. Liv and I were about seven when we watched *Saw* at a friend's house in utter nearly-sick shock, and my imagination henceforward always ran berserk. I've always hated jump-scares, but I'm drawn to them. There's a relief in just tipping the glass over and getting the inevitable out the way. It's probably part and parcel of being perennially on edge.

We called it The Dump because it was the huge pile of dirt right at the back of the garden behind the shed. There was a huge ivy archway dividing one part of the garden from another. It made the garden seem endless. In summer, if you stood inside the archway before passing through, you could hear the buzz of many bees, so I'd always leg it through for fear of being stung. Liv and I constructed a 'gym' made of plant pots and planks of wood back there once, and would pop up and down over the top of the fence dividing our garden and another young girl's over the way, as though we were performing some elaborate magic trick that showed the same person travelling at the speed of light to different areas of the fence. I think we thought that we were identical – to other people but not to each other.

The Dump had a kind of magnetism to us kids, maybe because we knew we weren't encouraged to go playing about in the dirt. Sometimes I'd find bird skulls there or in the flowerbeds and take them to my bedroom window-sill. One small skull I kept for a while, stroking the soft top and marvelling at the intricacy of its tiny jaw.

Bird

Though we always treated our fish well, it's hard to know if we weren't the ones who'd killed them. Our friend Amy's mam worried once that her fish was too cold so put it in warm water, which ended exactly as you'd imagine. Being weird and morbid as kids are, whenever I had a school friend over to play I'd dig the fish back out of The Dump and open the tissue to show them. The bird was different, though. It felt more alive than the fish did. They didn't change or do much other than swim this way and that and bob-bob with their little mouths. But the bird had grown before our very eyes, made it clear it needed us with its shrieks. I'd seen its little organs through skin sparked with tiny veins, and stroked his swollen belly so the thin skin wrinkled and moved under the pad of my finger. He was warm, alive. I wouldn't dig him back up. Turns out I wouldn't even get the chance. Not long after, the tree was felled to make way for the housing estate our closest childhood friend, Ashleigh, would end up living in.

I have no memory of taking the bird to the tree, who came, whether we said anything, how we dug the hole or how deep. I just know in my bones that that's where we put him, in our special place. Our place of infinite possibility.

I remember him with all the intensity of a child's experience, the desperate young love, guilt, the laughter and shouting, dismay and dirt, soggy tissue, brick and mortar. And a sinking feeling that, no matter how much I want to, I'll never be able to dig up the earth to find him.

2
Ketchup

All caravan sites are unique. To the untrained eye, sure, white and off-white static homes are most often regimentally lined up on promontories overlooking grey British beaches you'll never end up visiting because of the rain. You'll probably be able to hear the faint sound of a baby crying somewhere. There'll be a lukewarm swimming pool. An 'activity centre' of sorts, with a parched wooden dance floor on which grubby toddlers in nappies and tops will bob up and down, while Redcoats sing 'Star Trekkin''. There's probably a square of ceiling either mysteriously stained or dislodged, and the place smells of ale-soaked coasters and KP roasted peanuts. The lights of a one-armed bandit flash in the corner. Whenever I see one, I'm ruefully transported back to the time Liv and I, thrillingly unsupervised in some garish games room some way off from our caravan, grew so frustrated at the gambling machine we couldn't really reach that we shook it so hard the alarm started blaring. We legged it out of the musty old room, up the concrete bank and back to our caravan.

The familiarity of the experience was part of its draw, no doubt. After an hour or two the excitement of the journey turned into car-sickness relieved into a Wotsits packet, and incessant whining wanting to know if we were nearly there yet. Flipping through the CD case for what to listen to next was a powerful sensation. For one particular drive to a Scarborough-way resort, just Liv, Mam, Ashleigh and me, we'd burned our own CD using LimeWire. It was crudely done with some songs repeating and others not being quite what their title had promised. Not knowing quite what might accidentally sound through the car as the digital display switched from Track 5 to Track 6 added a dose of edgy excitement. We felt so grown up, puffing on candy cigarettes like 60-a-day broads beleaguered by life, and popping Parma Violets like pills.

We listened to Gigi D'Agostino's club banger *L'Amour Toujours* with the volume so loud the Golf's speakers buzzed with it. You'd think we were off our nuts high on a road trip through America rather than navigating the winding roads towards a grey seaside town. The childlike ring of the auto-tuned-to-death-robot-singer punched with a throbbing baseline conducive to throwing wild elbow-to-forearm shapes, like a film-set 'action' board snapping down and open again – a hungry Pac-Man spinning around, chomping its chops. We were hooked on the syrup river of the song, carried away on it, turning up the dial to its maximum to drown out Mam. And when for whatever unholy reason we were unable to replay the song (Mam's tanned hand obstructing the dial), what was this? Aly and AJ's 'Potential Breakup Song'? Oh yes bloody please. We'd listen to that a few hundred times. It was the perfect tune for Bratz-obsessed, drama-craving preteens. Instead of flailing in zigzags, we'd perform, miming the words in what was probably an overly sexual way for people so small. But we overflowed with sass! It was uncontainable. 'You're not living 'til you're living, living for me.' I still know all the words. After that was Green Day, Evanescence, and 'Untouched' by The Veronicas. Not a care in the world, apart from whether or not we were there yet. I don't think we stopped to think whether we actually wanted to get there, in that moment.

Families who'd met at the caravan site years ago would keep in touch, maybe arrange to return at the same time next year, perhaps even get caravans next to each other so the kids could play together. The adults could drink cheap wine while squeezed into the U-shaped couch at the far end of the caravan, rounded by net curtains and warmed by an old electric heater, listening to the tinny sound of rain on the roof. A damp dog lying at the faded doormat by the front door would howl to go out before sinking its head with a defeated whine onto its still-muddy front paws. There's always tomorrow.

We'd developed a relationship with a family like this before Mam and Dad divorced and moved a field's-length away from each other. There was an older blond lad called Lee, who looked a bit like a sexy Zuko from *Avatar: The Last Airbender*. If you know, you know. He was equally angsty, I recall. You know, a teenager. And as teenagers do, he acted like a teenager on top of being an actual teenager, emphasising his moody adolescence when around children younger than him.

It hadn't been at a caravan park, like, but some resort abroad, booked in the town-centre travel agents. Stepping inside that travel agent was stepping out of the real, grey-paved, pigeon-shit-stained world and into a paradise filled with the thick scent of artificial coconut. When you left, the smell was replaced by the pastries baking in the Cooplands next door. Anyway, there was also a younger boy called Lewis, who must've only been two. He had the cheekiest chubby face and huge brown eyes and was a living doll for Liv and I to fawn over. We'd sit on their sunbeds and play Lee's chunky purple Game Boy, our white necks protected by flaps on the back of our caps, little white legs visible under the oversized T-shirts we'd wear into the pool, too, running across the hot floor back to the sunbeds when we were done, swaddled in colourful towels.

We only visited them once, or maybe it was twice, that I can remember – all the way in Chester. We must've only been five or six, Liv and I, and the drive seemed interminable. I was disappointed when we got there and it was just a drab suburban house not dissimilar to those at home, if a bit bigger than ours. I remained completely in love with Lee, who obviously saw me as the child that I was. It was the kind of desperate love confused with exciting new surroundings. Even going on holiday in Freshers' with my new university friends to Berlin made my friend Callum, who I've only ever loved as a Best Best Friend, seem like a solid prospect. It's hard to love a city. There's nothing physical, really, to latch onto. It's the feeling, the *vibe*, that grabs you and in your new-experience goggles you project that onto the unlucky person who happens to be with you.

It happened before that Freshers' trip, too, when I was 18 and on my first girls' holiday to Ibiza. I became utterly obsessed with a blond (theme?) Scouser with a receding hairline who was one of our reps. I could barely focus on my copy of *Catch-22*, in case he at any moment came over to our sunbeds to ask if we were up for the boat party, which, I guess, yeah – hair curled behind my ear subtly, throat cleared – I guess that sounds cool. He made it clear when we flirted that he wasn't allowed to get with clients, but after throwing eyes at him across the all-inclusive hotel buffet of rubbery calamari and unexplained pasta dishes and chips, I threw myself at him at a glow-stick party when I was off my face on sugary alcopops and suspect cocktails. Someone else from Billingham turned out to be in that very bar for that very party, which kind of dampened the mood and we had to leave early so one of us could go vomit, but ah, those summer nights! Elsewhere on the strip we walked past a bar throbbing with the chant 'T-T-Teessiders'. You can take the girl out of Teesside, but the region's influence is, apparently, global – as the saying goes.

At a Radio 1 DJ set on our last night, our hands brushed. He squeezed my hand in his and it was warm and clammy and forbidden and the music was thumping like the blood in my ears. I was in ecstasy. Continuing the stalking, I added him on Facebook and we exchanged a few cringey messages. He said he was going to come and visit me, but I thought we'd both seem different if we weren't in the sun. With him back at his mam's in Liverpool and me back at my mam's in Billingham, the initial lustre disappeared like Klingande's 'Jubel' from the charts that year. A saxophone's music fading into the distance. It didn't help that he used the winky-face so often I got the ick.

But Lee was before social media, and our exchanges were over Swingball in their modest Chester back garden. Other than the fact I lost my first milk tooth on that trip, and that I woke up with five pound coins (five! Mam!) under my pillow, I don't really remember anything else about it. Well, other than crying all the way home because I didn't want to leave my uninterested, inappropriately aged paramour.

Once, abroad in Greece – don't worry, we'll be back in Skegness soon – Liv and I were both smitten by a pair of fellas in their early twenties who played with us in the pool and kept an eye on us when Mam was asleep on the sunbed. Before we left, they presented us each with a plastic brown and cream beaded necklace we interpreted as a clear sign they loved us too. When we went home, we sat on Mam's double bed and cried and cried for them, necklaces crutched like rosaries in our fists. Their short-sleeved oversized shirts, their hairy tanned legs, hair spiked up with thick, wet gel, eyes framed by the kind of mirrored faux-sporting sunglasses you find on a spinning rack at a service station. Losing them felt like the end of summer.

It had all been very innocent stuff. But it changed when we were 12 or 13 and Liv, Mam, Ashleigh (our pseudo-adopted daughter) and I went to a hotel in Turkey. The smattering of white, flat-topped buildings was punctuated by palm trees. Mam drank and we plunged into the freezing cold pool every day, laughing and shivering as we broke the surface and wriggle-swam to keep warm. A curly-haired dreamboat of a man – though now I think he must've been seventeen or maybe eighteen – started lingering around the pool trying to play with us. But after the initial intrigue it wasn't really fun and we felt awkward. Liv and I were always blessed with a pool companion in each other, though we did make friends with other kids in the pool for games that required more than two, or because their beach ball had accidentally floated over to us and one thing led to another. Here, though, not only did we have each other as per usual, we had our Ash, and we were getting to the age where kids are more self-aware and thus less likely to declare themselves unselfconsciously as a stranger's fast friend. But that wasn't why we felt awkward.

This man didn't really speak much English (probably couldn't) and we couldn't speak Turkish – a fair enough state of affairs but one that, compounded by his weird behaviour, made his muteness eerie. What weird behaviour, you ask? Well, he pushed us in the pool a little too forcefully, held our heads under the water for a second longer than was strictly comfortable, and splashed us with his strong forearm in large sweeping motions. I started feeling wary, turning around to see if he was about, just out of the corner of my peripheral vision, I don't know if out of excitement or anticipation or what. He'd burst our bubble and it was thrilling, but … we no longer had a bubble. If I turned around and he wasn't there, I'd feel a jolt of relief-mingled disappointment.

One warm evening as we were walking around the pool (into which a stray kitten fell one day, which we dutifully fished out before it drowned), he handed me a small note as we approached the bar. He leaned against a tall circular table. Waiting. Looking. When we got back to our own table with our drinks, I unfolded it and it was a phone number. At least I assumed it was. It wasn't the usual 07 or +44 I was used to, and I immediately panicked that maybe it would cost a fortune to send even a short message to it. I already knew I was going to text it, I suppose, compulsively. I had to look, even if I wasn't supposed to. Especially because I wasn't supposed to.

I felt weird, at once exhilarated and fearful, baffled by the number and the complicated logistics it seemed to present. It was like some kind of animal instinct kicked in. He was looking over. I can't remember ever seeing him with anyone else there. Maybe he wasn't, on reflection, even holidaying at the hotel, but had just opted to be my shadow. I turned my back to him and enjoyed the rest of our night, filled to the brim with all the stars in the sky.

Mam teased and elbow nudged 'Ee, Tilly,' (she's always called me Tilly, meaning for whatever unknown reason someone full of mischief) 'you've got an admirer!' I felt so seen: naked, appreciated, spotlighted. His eyes bore into the back of my head, and when I turned around he was gone.

The next day, full of nauseating trepidation, I texted him off Mam's phone. We didn't yet have our own, were too young. He replied fast. I felt uncomfortable, vaguely afraid, but I couldn't help myself. Also, what would happen if I didn't message the number he'd so surreptitiously passed me before disappearing into the night? The speed of his response indicated he'd been waiting for me to text. That, or he was addicted to his phone, but back then it didn't have a suite of addictive social media, or probably even a camera, just Snake. In any case, I was plagued by a looming sense of danger. He thought I was pretty, etcetera. It felt innocuous and sweet, every text momentarily dispelling some anxiety before the inevitable pause before another one flashed onto the screen. When we left he said he was sorry to see me go, and would I add him on MSN? When I got back to the UK I did – out of curiosity-mixed compulsion as much as anything. The holiday had worn off, I was a safe and manageable distance away from him, and we chatted a bit.

My enormous ego also probably had something to do with it. In primary school I was completely obsessed with being fancied. Ob. Sessed. Maturing earlier than most of my peers, lumpy little tit mounds coming in far earlier than anyone would choose, I became aware early on that I was, that I could be, an object of adoration and attraction. As someone who craves undying affection, it was a marvellous revelation, and I, like a modern-day working-class Cleopatra, went to great lengths to expand my influence as far and wide as possible. I'd go around all the boys in my year group, which wasn't many, and ask them outright whether they fancied me. The cheek! But it worked. Well, it seemed like it worked. Eventually I managed to get a full score – all of the boys said they fancied me – but on reflection it may very well have been that they were terrified by the intense look in my eyes as I approached them, again, at playtime. I'd tell Liv and whoever would listen that *all* the boys fancied me, that they'd told me themselves. I didn't intend to do anything with the information, mind, other than cruelly ensure everyone was helplessly in love with me.

It was just such an ego that blinded me to the fact I was accidentally but almost definitely speaking to a pervert on MSN once, using Mam's bulky computer in the dining room. A celebrity had invited me to connect, for God's sake! MC Smally, of 'Guna go by the flow, guna play the game' fame. MC Smally – who, like DJ Boonie, was part of the collective playlist of our adolescence – wanted to talk to *me*. In Years 7 to 8 we'd all go to the Billingham Forum dressed up to the nines, get on our chunky navy-and-red-laced Forum-issue ice skates, and skate in circles to songs like Special D's 'Come With Me'. I'd spend less time on the ice and more time, tightly booted up, in the corner with my young beau, who kissed like a horny washing machine. I loved it. I kissed like a horny washing machine back. Maybe I'd eventually get to kiss DJ Smally in a similar manner if I played this right. It started when someone with the username DJ Smally had followed me on MSN and said he was a friend of a friend and did I like his music? I do! I'm a huge fan! (I wasn't, really – only joke-liked the song because knowing all the words was fun). I excitedly told Liv I was instant messaging *MC effing Smally*. Could she believe? Turns out, she could not, and told me it was most likely a random nonce and that I should block them immediately. So, begrudgingly, I did, but was it really so damn hard to believe I could be the object of a celebrity's attraction?

I was, after all, destined for great things myself. As a kid with an empty space where confidence should've been, and who genuinely couldn't imagine her life past 22 (the ancient, adult age my mam's brother had been when he took his own life), in the burgeoning awareness of my complex consciousness I thought I spied exceptionalism. I had thoughts of my own, ideas about the world around me; surely that meant I was special? I had to be special. I was desperate to be special. It didn't occur to me that I was just going through the various stages of childhood and adolescent development, was learning things about myself and the world around me like every fucker else. No, I was the first person to achieve object permanence. Invented it. I had a whole world bubbling in me always; surely that had to count for something? Liv, on the other hand, has always exuded a quiet, self-assured confidence that is her brilliant bedrock. She didn't and still doesn't need to be gobby, to peacock around telling everyone how many boys fancy her.

Her direct, annoying contrast, I had to be adored, set apart. I think this was, paradoxically, a symptom less of confidence and rather of a lack thereof. I needed validating at all times, I was a crumbling scaffold of a thing; Liv was a building. No matter how confidently I postured, it was clear who would fall if an earthquake hit. Even small tremors threatened my very foundations, but she's Vesuvius-proof.

Being fanciable was, I think, a way of trying to control my surroundings, of being *sure* about things. No maybes, no I think sos tacked onto the end of sentences, no mounting anticipation of when I'd inevitably spill my drink at tea and get in trouble. I sensed even then that in womanhood there was a power, and for someone who felt so completely helpless all the time it was scintillating.

Likewise did I approach academic and any other kind of success where I could grab it. I deludedly thought – a belief defiantly embedded in me even now – that once I was 'on top' I wouldn't need to feel so anxious any more, because I'd be on top and have a bird's-eye view over everything. Life wouldn't be so unpredictable, and even if it was, I'd be way above it all. Untouchable, imperturbable. For someone who felt, feels, trapped in a maze, the idea of being able to see it from above – to see just how everyone else seems to be making their way through so well when you alone can't – is *everything*. I'd be flying among the sun-struck clouds, free to breathe. A mirage, of course. Once I was wheeling high above everyone else, I'd only find something else to worry about. The clouds aren't puffy enough, the sun's too bright, I feel *too* free up here. God, can I get a refund? I need to fly higher! Why can't I fly higher? Oh Icarus, you poor bairn.

I realise now that all I've ever wanted is security, and for a preteen me that meant one thing: becoming a famous singer. That was my escape route to the dazzling heights I thought I craved. Luckily, in Year 9 St Michael's was having a talent competition, and my friend Jenny and I auditioned in our dull maths classroom in front of Year 11s. It was terrifying, and my voice shook. On the advice of Jenny's mam, we decided to call our band of two 'Because', because – and this is the clever part – we could say when asked why it was called that, 'just because'. Little bit of attitude, why the hell not. We sang a song by the Sugababes and got through.

My gran, Mam's mam, has always known I've a pretty decent singing voice and was delighted to hear I'd made it to the next round. But I had such crippling stage fright that I immediately got cold feet; the news we'd made it through made my stomach turn. Trying to help me dispel my fear of singing in front of other people, Gran came over and sat on the edge of my bed and told me just to sing to her. She was just one person, and she wouldn't judge me harshly. I couldn't, so she swivelled and said,

'OK, let's try with my back to you.' Wait, did my gran accidentally invent *The Voice*? Anyway, there she sat, waiting, and I sang 'Heaven' by DJ Sammy. I can't remember her reaction or what happened next, only that I didn't perform in the talent show, which incidentally was called The X Factor. Apparently unfazed that I'd never and could never sing in front of other people, I wanted with an aching burning passion to go on the actual *X Factor* and win. To understand why, please refer back to the paragraph in your manuals about a crippling need for worldwide unconditional love.

I'd seen early on that even Jesus didn't get that, and things didn't exactly turn out amazingly for him, but my childish semi-god-complex was, unlike every other aspect of my young psyche, unshaken. No, I'd sit on YouTube in the living room when Liv was out and Mam was upstairs and pull up Israel Kamakawiwo'ole's 'Somewhere Over the Rainbow (Instrumental)' and sing my heart out. Sometimes it would be Whitney's 'I Will Always Love You' (an ambitious choice entirely out of mine or anyone else's range) or 'My Heart Will Go On', known to us as 'The Titanic Song'. God knows what our neighbours thought. No garlands of congratulatory flowers or cookie bouquets landed on our doorstep, nor any press, so maybe He did have some idea.

After one particular episode of *The X Factor*, I ran upstairs to my bedroom, plonked myself on Liv's bed (at every single opportunity, I went in her bed; if she was out, I'd nap there; sleeping over Ash's, I'd sleep there. Liv's smell. Liv's bed. Liv), pressed my face into her pillow and cried and cried and cried. The tears streamed down my face and it was the kind of heaving cry that leaves you dramatically gasping for breath. My mam, completely baffled by what was even for me a very strange reaction to a show we'd both just enjoyed together, came up and perched on the edge of the bed, rubbing my back affectionately. When she asked me what was up, I eventually (after a few failed 'go away's) turned my blotchy, streaked face to her, caught my breath and managed to get out, 'I just want to win *The X Factor*,' after which I duly erupted into another fit of tragic, body-strewn-over-a-chaise-longue lamentation.

Back on MSN, the Turkish man from holiday told me he was 18 and quickly started to explain what he'd like me to do to him. I was so shocked I immediately blocked him. The strange powder we had in the bathroom at home reminded me of him. It had a little wooden scoop on it and looked like talc. A cylindrical cap was slid upwards to get it off, and the container was decorated red and black, with little cartoon characters that could've been Japanese. Was it some kind of bath salt? I don't know. I've never seen it anywhere since and have no idea how it got into our bathroom, or why. Maybe it was perfectly innocuous, or maybe he'd given me it as a gift, but every time I smelled it I was transported to thoughts of him lingering around the pool; his gorgeous curls and golden skin; his texts; his lewd, misspelt blowjob messages. I was glad to no longer be in the Turkish sun.

Most of our package holidays have been mushed into one big bulging memory. All the oceans just one wide ocean. The smell of coconut mingled with the glorious stench of stale cigarette smoke (even now, walking past a smoking area reminds me of parasols and tiny plastic tubs of finger-scooped Nutella pilfered from a 'continental' breakfast spread). The time we went to a Wild West-themed waterpark is the same as the time Dad took our flour-filled stretchy potato head toy (it was latex skin with googly eyes and a pathetic tuft of hair, full of flour and kneadable, like bread) and stretched it until it blew an enormous white cloud all over him.

Once, on this apparent mega-holiday, Liv, Mam and I were walking back to the hotel. The air is always different abroad – you can just feel it the second you step off the plane and the heat hits you like a wall. That night it was thick and navy and warm. A cloudless sky stretched enormous above us and hundreds of glinting stars could be seen whichever way you turned. Suddenly, a thin silver slither sliced the sky before disappearing absolutely into the canvas. Blink and you'd miss it, but we didn't. Liv and I were the type of amazed that only events like these can leave you: learning about volcanoes and earthquakes, about space, the dinosaurs, the *Titanic*, Pompeii. Utterly enthralled by a phenomenon that blew my tiny mind, Mam set about disclosing all her adult knowledge about shooting stars and meteors.

My wonderment soured to panic. *What do you mean, sometimes they just* fall *to the earth? How on earth are any of you adults just walking around like nothing has happened when at any moment a literal bit of sky could literally fall on top of your head and kill you? Are you out of your minds?*

This utter disbelief was akin to when, much later, I found out what sex was and couldn't for the life of me understand how people went about their daily business knowing that they'd seen another person *naked* and done *that*. How they looked in the eye any of the people they'd, you know, fucked. For weeks afterwards, I felt bashful even looking at my teachers, knowing that they had probably done it, and were acting like they hadn't! Were they thinking about it right now? As an adult, I now realise there was a distinct possibility they were, in the middle of teaching biology, thinking about their latest decent shag. But probably not in the mind-consuming way I'd imagined they were, I admit.

So here we are, walking under the stars, and I become deathly afraid that at any moment a meteorite is going to fall on my head before we get back to the hotel. My action was a tried and tested classic: cry until you're heaving for breath between sobs, like you're watching *Titanic* for the first time and Rose has to live the rest of her life without Jack, and after doing *that* with him in the sweaty vintage car!

As ever, Mam consoled me to the best of her ability, trying hard to penetrate my fog of existential ennui and snot bubbles with sense. 'The chances of one actually falling on you and hitting you are basically non-existent.'

'Basically?' I retorted. Smart arse. 'So you're saying it *could* happen?'

Momentarily forgetting which sunbed is yours after breaking the pool's surface, temporarily blinded by water and a hot beating sun, panicking because you've come up at an unexpected angle and can't see your parents – these are not experiences you need to jump on a plane for. In truth, you don't even need to go to a caravan park. Letting go of your mam's hand in Woolworth's has (had, RIP) the same effect. It's very much a part of the caravanning experience, too. The pain is much less localised, however, since the parents are the ones burdened with finding their way back.

It was inevitable, on one of these holidays, that for the first couple of days you'd frequently forget where exactly your caravan was 'parked', in a sea of nightmarishly identical caravans that made finding the Golf in the Tesco car park mere child's play. The arguments, tantrums, snotty noses, ducking and weaving with arms thrown back for optimum aerodynamism through makeshift streets. There'd always be a hill you had to walk up, too – an essential part of the package promised in the glossy brochures. 'We've already been this way around. We passed that same gnome, there, David.' (Pre-divorce, faint and distant voices.) 'That gnome there!'

To a child, these places were Wonderland: the unusual blend of possibility and mundanity found in airports, the select number of small shops containing keyrings and goggles, five-pound holiday coupons cut out of the *Sun*, the promise of novelty.

And the pièce de résistance: the Restaurant. Plates of turkey dinosaurs, potato smileys and beans wolfed down by littl'uns; microwaved lasagne with a sprig of 'erb for the adults. Tiny hands gripping forks like shovels, tomato juice drying sticky and hastily scrubbed with a tissue by Mam before a ball pit is dived into: red, yellow and blue balls that swallowed kids whole. It was an intense place, and its uniqueness lay underfoot in the form of a garish patterned carpet. Adults in Barnaby Bear costumes would harass families as they ate and made the children cry.

If you've not yet gathered, I was a pretty anxious child. I once misunderstood my gran saying I was accident-prone after I stumbled on a tree root in John Whitehead Park and scuffed my knees, thinking she'd called me an accident prawn. I barrelled through space with a maniacal giggle and chaotic energy, once on a holiday abroad knocking a whole shelf of wine in a tiny shop crashing to the floor. Wherever I went there'd be the wobbly sound of a rushed-past spinning vase settling back into place.

During one of these meals, I felt an overwhelming urge. The kind I'd tried to explain to Mam once, hanging off the arm of her yellow sofa: 'Is it normal to have a voice in your head telling you to do things over and over until you do?' I was always told off for spilling stuff, which was inevitable, to the point where waiting for it to happen became too much and I'd tip my glass just to get it out of the way, to dispel the tension. Now, I could feel it build-ing. The sachets of condiments were taunting me, so I sneaked a ketchup and tottered to the bathroom with it up a snot-crusted sleeve.

Once in the cubicle – which I locked, despite fearing I'd get stuck in there forever and would be dead by the time the fire brigade came to cut the door off, which, to be honest, would be a good thing because I'd only die of embarrassment otherwise – I pulled out the surreptitious sauce and held it in my hands like a maniacal Frankenstein, awe-struck by what he saw before him.

I started to squeeze, the compulsion easing (sweet relief, a pressure valve opens) as ecstasy built, each twist edging me, us, closer and closer, the packet a ballooning hour-glass, each orb of eight getting thicker until – POP! A bright red explosion in all directions.

I only remember the moment it exploded. I can't remember what happened next, have probably repressed it. I hated getting bollocked, still do. Most likely I sat on the closed toilet seat for a bit, contemplating what I'd done and weighing up the precise extent of the bollocking I was likely to get. I've no doubt I was as ketchup-splattered as the white walls of the cubicle. And I no doubt panicked that someone had heard and thought my tummy had reacted badly to the potato smiles. Maybe some kind stranger knocked to ask if everything was 'OK, chick?' Did I wonder why I'd done it? It didn't seem as complicated then as it does now. I had tension and I released it; what was there to think about? I didn't regret it, I know that much. Maybe I'd held it away from me to minimise the damage I knew I was about to do. Did I scrub the cubicle clean with one-ply tissue paper, or did I leave it? I wouldn't want to say, lest I get a tummy ache.

My compulsions were random, like an imaginary friend urging me irresistibly to do different things. A game of Simon Says with a malevolent Simon hell-bent on doing my head in. My mind just felt, even at six or seven, *wrong*. Maybe I was confusing the inner voice everyone has – literal consciousness – with something separate from myself. Again, throwing my belly over the sofa, legs bent and swinging behind me, I'd asked Mam whether it was normal not to look on the outside how I felt on the inside. I can't remember her response. I'm sure it was lovely and well-meaning, but I don't think it helped.

It was like I was too aware that there was a person inside my body, and I was therefore watching myself doing stuff, narrating my life like an overactive Morgan Freeman. *You may be wondering how I got here.* I still do it. Maybe it's my imagined God, watching me in case I say I want strawberry ice cream when I really want chocolate and striking me with a belly-ache specific lightning bolt for being such a lying heathen. It wasn't a fun *Drop Dead Fred* scenario, unfortunately. I didn't literally have an imaginary friend (didn't need one, had Liv). The urges would just come unbidden, random. *Bite down really, really hard on your front teeth. Stick your fingers down your throat until you gag. Hold your breath.* Not like our friend Sarah used to do when she was a kid (she'd hold her breath until she got her own way), since I wasn't trying to achieve anything beyond satisfying my internal tormenter. He'd only come up with something new and even weirder after. Bastard. *You've got to go make sure all the cutlery on the kitchen table is perfectly straight. Turn the light off with your tongue instead of your finger* (not proud of that one). *Stare at the sun. Squeeze that ketchup sachet until it pops.*

I wonder whether those white walls still bear any unique trace of my weird act. No caravan park is the same, after all.

3
Bed

I've always been a nervous sleeper. It didn't help that when Liv and I were around 11 years old she was utterly demonic in the night. We'd talk in bed after lights out, sometimes cracking each other up to the point of belly aches and tears, sometimes speculating on the existence of aliens (most probable). I wasn't able to sleep unless the last thing I'd said, and she'd said to me, was 'Night, love you,' in case I died in my sleep. *In case I died in my sleep*. An infuriating little ritual. At that age I absorbed information like triple-ply kitchen roll soaking up tea rings. Undoubtedly, I'd overheard some adult TV about people dying in their sleep and convinced myself it would happen to me. I also had to know the exact time I was going to sleep – impossible, really, to ascertain. I'd ask what time it was, Liv would give a vague summation, rounded to the hour or half hour or quarter hour, and I'd say 'No, the exact time,' and she'd say 'For God's sake, it's 10:08, Lauren, you're such a freak.' No wonder she started acting like a child possessed after I nightly created such a morbid environment for us to drop off into.

My imagination did a lot of overtime, worrying about insignificant this and that. Liv's did too, evidently. She'd have a recurring nightmare – now likely to be replaced by the immortalisation of it in print, sorry Liv – about being a small pink Lego piece that was being consumed by larger Lego pieces. So far so cute. But every Sunday night at around the same time it'd happen, that same hell of primary colours and cuboids with gaping mouths. It became so like clockwork she'd get upset before bed, crying because she didn't want to have the dream. Some people have a 'dream house' that's not the same layout or often completely dissimilar to their actual house, but which they return to time and time again in sleep. Others a beloved literary landscape they can step into after years away and nothing has changed – the Manderley you've always seen in your mind's eye. Like a dreamscape, I can still see my rendering of that ghastly Lego hell. I wonder if Liv can too. I understood something of the skin-prickling terror she experienced. Once I had a temperature so high that I hallucinated the bricks of the house were falling in on me, without end.

Later, when the Lego dream stopped – or at least, she stopped mentioning it – Liv started sitting up in her sleep, sometimes with her eyes open. I'd wake up and there would be, with her long hair falling low, the girl from *The Ring* sitting bolt upright in silence. Although sometimes I was too spooked to intervene lest she reveal fangs or eyes of pure obsidian, on other occasions I woke her with a frantic 'Liv! Liv! Liv!' to which she'd woozily, confusedly come round and tuck herself back in. Sometimes it was just a raised arm, arguably worse to be honest, or a rogue leg. Like some invisible puppeteer had got bored halfway through 'The Lonely Goatherd'. Without Julie Andrews it's just a bit ominous – more blasted heath than matching dungarees.

On the plus side, at least these spectral callisthenics only distressed one of us. At first. But then she started walking downstairs and setting the alarm off. Like a spooky baby she had to crawl and squirm before she took her first steps, but step she did. This distressed all of us. It hurt my heart as much as it shocked me awake, because at the midnight scream of the rudimentary alarm system she'd be just as scared as me.

When we were teenagers and staying at Dad and Ruth's house over the field, I awoke one night to Liv's radgy, hushed voice. The attic had been turned into a bedroom for us, up a winding set of stairs with no door at the bottom – the stairs the vestige of our young privacy. It had a brilliant roof window, and my teenage boyfriends and I would look out wistfully at star-twinkled night skies that rotated almost as fast as they did, with Big Michael's cylindrical flats always square in the middle of the frame. Liv shout-whispered, 'Lauren, give me my quilt back, I swear to God it's not funny.' It took me a while to realise what was going on through the gauzy haze of sleep. 'What are you on about, Liv? Why the hell would I steal your quilt?' Dying for this charade to be over and for her to realise she'd just kicked it off the side or something, I, naturally fearful of someone grabbing my hand from underneath my bed, tentatively dropped a hand to feel for her quilt around the bed. Nothing. 'Liv, man.' I don't know why I didn't just turn the light on; we had the most perfect oblivion-inducing blackout blind. I swiped away her egregious suggestion of theft and told her I couldn't feel it anywhere around our beds.

Frustrated, we finally turned the light on, her jaw clenched in an annoyance soon shaken as we both discovered that the bright pink quilt was, in fact, gone. I was, obviously, immediately terrified. What kind of sick pervert breaks into a house only to steal a young girl's quilt? It didn't bear thinking about. And then – God, no, please – a skin-creeping violin-ascending question formed. Was he still here? The boiler was tucked behind the plaster wall that formed a part of the loft renovation and it often dripped and groaned and creaked ominously, and much to my dismay a row of floor-level cupboards opened into a 'tunnel' that skirted round the edge of the room. The perfect hiding place for any child playing hide-and-seek with a serial killer who has a shotgun while the house is also on fire. We scrambled to the top of the stairs to bravely peer over the banister, two floppy-haired heads. At the bottom of the stairs her pink quilt was pooled. It was not, as suspected, draped around the shoulders of a balaclava-clad man, turning him into some odd-looking superhero. Rather, Liv had thrown the single duvet down the stairs in her sleep and put herself back to bed. Her indignant expression broke into a stubborn, laughing smile. I probably laughed an 'Oh my God,' and rolled my eyes with a 'You absolute doyle' as we both walked the few steps back to bed.

Perhaps all children know something of the vulnerability of night-time, of sleep. A latent flame at first, soon fanned by playground stories of burglaries and home invasions real and imagined. And the one we've all heard, about the person thinking that their hand, falling off the edge of the bed in repose, was being licked by a dog only to find *there had never been a dog*. But Liv and I were always, I think, a bit more restless, especially with Mam being mentally unwell and prone to behaving unusually at times. To a child's mind that can just mean being up late, but sometimes its the irrational belief that the house has been rigged with cameras. In my case this restlessness manifested itself in fear that I'd die in my sleep. Saying 'Night, love you' almost became preventative, a mantra that if forgotten would prove fatal. Even now, living hundreds of miles apart, I text her last thing, or she me, and we know what it means.

I used to ask our childhood friend Ashleigh, you know Ashleigh, *constantly* whether I was her best friend. Because there's never been a tactic more absolutely successful to securing friendship than holding someone hostage by it. I knew I was, her best friend that is, but I just had to hear the words come from her mouth. The only difference with Liv was that I inherently knew she was my best friend. Know she is.

Though we were indubitably a trio, Liv and Ash were assigned the same form at secondary school – H in the MICHAEL while I was the E – and were *best* friends in the sense of two people who have chosen each other, as opposed to the best friend I was, in the more general sense. I'd fear that I only had friends because I was inextricably tied to Liv and she had friends, and I projected the worst of it onto poor Ash. We'd watch the latest music videos on the computer that used to sit in the corner of Mam's living room when we were just starting out at big school – its bulky, overheating tower alongside a monitor bearing sticky finger marks. After Matt Cardle won *The X Factor*, Liv was utterly obsessed with the man, to the point of wearing a T-shirt with his face on for bed. She'd moved on from Jamiroquai, whose CD played often on our faded blue boombox, surrounded on the floor by hair straighteners and stray bobby pins. Before school we'd watch the bootcamp video of him singing 'The First Time Ever I Saw Your Face', which to her credit was goosebumps angelic, and other music videos of the songs we liked at the time. Our Freeview did have a couple of music channels, and E4 at that time did big themed countdowns and played chart hits, but YouTube meant we could listen as many times as we needed for Liv and Ash to nail the routines they'd choreograph. The best they ever did was to 'Club Can't Handle Me' by Flo Rida; we rewound it so many times to get them in sync that I still know all the words

I don't know why I never joined in. It wasn't that I didn't like dancing – on the contrary, at primary school only a year earlier we'd all three of us lead the morning 'Wake Up Shakeup' dance everyone would do in the playground before our first class. With the self-assurance and smugness gleaned simply from being the oldest in the school, five or six of us confidently stood facing the road that ran along the edge of the yard and led routines to '5,6,7,8' by Steps and the like, the music blaring from a boombox placed on the concrete, awkwardly pulled through the window. Maybe I just liked to watch the two of them dance. The living room was only wide enough for two people throwing the moves they were throwing anyway. Perhaps I was too busy perfecting my heavily backcombed hair with Mam's hairspray and comb, so it was nigh on rock solid and didn't move (just one more spray, just in case) on the grey, oftentimes blustery walk to school.

My irresistible urge for open, constant affection and reassurance extended to St Michael's dinnertime. Me and Liv were on free school meals, and the meagre budget meant you could get two out of the three things on offer: a drink, a dessert and a meal. She and Ash paired up every day – there was no question, that was the way things went – and I was self-righteously aggrieved that I should have to choose, when they shared a drink, and each got a dessert and main. I'd therefore sneak a crumbling brownie up my worn sleeve, picking out fabric-caught specks instead of paying attention in next period.

I was never naughty in any excessive – catchable – sense (she says, having just admitted to literal confectionary thieving). Other pupils jumped out the first-floor window when the teacher wasn't looking and pegged it round the corner where people smoked. Someone might put a single bollock on a teacher's keyboard while they were in the staffroom. A group of lads who called themselves 'The Lynch Mob' once locked a boy in the toilets and he was only let out after a dinner lady heard his increasingly desperate 'It's not funny any more!' bangs on the door. We all cheered when he was let out. The single cubicles in there were absolutely tiny. I remember sitting in one listening to the rain pound down on the ceiling and wondering whether, as I had heard on the grapevine, the Mayans really had cracked it and the world was going to end that day. The sudden turn in the weather seemed to confirm it; no one played in the link-fenced AstroTurf outside the houseblock that day, so sodden was it with pools of rain.

This self-proclaimed Lynch Mob, who to my knowledge weren't called out nearly half as publicly and loudly as such a vile moniker deserves, would hide behind the fence of the depressing memorial garden (I can't remember who it memorialised) and grab unsuspecting people who walked past, pulling them over the fence and onto the floor. I nearly got scooped up once, but I didn't mind too much because I fancied one of them. I never faced the kind of ordeal experienced by the little fat boy who was chased around the field panting for his life, catapulted through a fence when he was caught.

Sure, I stole brownies to be like Liv and Ash and because I wanted one and thought it unfair I couldn't have one just because I didn't have the money. And sure, if I bought a raffle ticket I'd sometimes purposefully pick out of the wrong bag (the one that had all the previous winning tickets in, all ending in 0s and 5s), feigning confusion that the Easter egg attached to ticket number 15 had already been taken, only to be given another one. It didn't occur to me that the consolation egg I got meant someone else's ticket would result in no prize, since it would by then be in my belly, nor that an almost life-sized Jesus on the cross loomed over the hall and saw it all. But really, I was polite in class and did my work, and to my credit didn't catapult anyone through any fences. The bar I'm setting here is, admittedly, *low*.

The deputy head teacher looked like the slug who says 'Wazowski, you didn't file your paperwork' in *Monsters Inc*. She'd been there even when Dad and his brothers had been at the school, and she resented how I looked. My skin was forever a fading patchwork of cheap instant tan, the white of my school collar daubed orange and brown. If I'd just buttoned up the top button (which would've been social suicide) I'd probably have got away with it, but it flopped open for all to see. The barely tied tie – a trend I still cannot understand, but the thicker the 'knot' the better, apparently – did not conceal the grubby, baked-in marks.

Also against the dress code, by Year 9 I had a pixie cut with the sides shaved. OK, it was also dyed using bright red dye that made Mam's bathroom look like a crime scene. I wore lashings of mascara, first on lashes I'd cut using nail scissors so they could be short and stubby like the popular girls' lashes, and then, when I came to my senses, on long, spidery lashes. Once, Mrs *Monster's Inc.* called Liv and me into her office to demand we remove our make-up *that very second*. Thrust a baby wipe, I reluctantly went to work on my mascara and kohl-lined eyes. Liv, quiet as ever, did the same on hers, and she showed the remarkably clean wipe to the teacher. Her eyelashes were so long and thick and full that the teacher had mistakenly thought she'd been wearing mascara. As she left the office, it was all I could to do to hold in an eruptive 'Fuck yeah!' and jump into the air, *Breakfast Club*-style.

Liv's eyes are insane. She has heterochromia, which means they're different colours, like David Bowie's and some cats' eyes. In all the baby pictures they're of course blue, but slowly they began to change until one was brown with a fleck of blue and the other green, like my mam's. They're also big as a bug's eyes, and lined with sky-reaching lashes that make her look like a doll. When we were little and on holiday, Mam had to shield her from grasping hands and a trail of 'ooh's. Meanwhile, I stood squat, pre-hair dye and make-up, like a miniature Wayne Rooney. I've of course teased her for the sake of it, calling her 'alien' and 'bong-eye', before finally landing on 'Bong-eyed Steve,' who she remains to this day.

As is my birthright. If anyone else dared say anything about her, I was all over them like a rash. Surprisingly, I never actually had a fight at school, despite a burgeoning anger problem and, well, puberty, but I saw plenty of hair-grabbing scraps between girls in the bus bays after school. One rumour had it that a girl in Year 11 had once stabbed someone in the face with the heel of her shoe, but heels weren't allowed so she was either an off-the-rails renegade or the story was bullshit. All you'd need to see against the green of the field between the school and the bus bays was a hive of navy-jumpered bodies huddled and jostling this way and that like a swarm of bees to realise a fight had broken out. Also, someone always shouted 'Fight!' to get the crowd in. I got close once, though. A girl we weren't friends with had called Liv 'bong-eyed' (*Excuse me?*) and I saw red, confronting her – flanked by our friendship group – in front of the science block one break time. 'You don't fucking say anything about Liv,' I spat. 'Do you understand?'

My anxiety around whether I had any friends, which persists to this day, never really extended to Liv. Of course, I'd have preferred her to lavish me constantly with the adoration I believed was my womb-sharer's privilege, but she and I found comfort in each other's presence – our relationship, if unspoken, nevertheless God-given. Once, we pushed our single beds together so we could sleep in a double bed, getting a double duvet to complete the trans-formation. When I went to university and spent my first ever night away from her – apart from the short stint when, tired of my crap, she moved into the tiny spare bedroom at Mam's house – I hated it.

For one thing, I was scared of the dark. Being constantly full of mischief, I'd try and scare her as we tried to fall asleep in our single beds at Mam's, asking her what she'd do if there was a man in the wardrobe right now. 'You're only scaring yourself, Lauren.' She was right, of course. Even our innocent mental explorations of the night sky and the probability of extraterrestrial life eventually scared me. I'd have to smooth the curtains so there were no cracks or creases that someone, however impossibly thin, could hide behind. When I went away, I wasn't used to not having someone to whisper to before bed. I was used to knowing she was there, even if she was deathly quiet. I knew it was her coming up the stairs even if she didn't say a word. It broke my heart. I still miss not being able to hear her, if not see her, moving around our space, coming up the stairs, brushing her teeth.

Even now, years later, I still sleep like I'm on the first shift. The slightest bump in the night and I'll shoot up, immediately wrenched out of sleep, babbling 'Liv, Liv, Liv, Liv, Mam, Mam, Mam,' as though someone were taking them away.

Before any of this, I had the same fear for myself. When I was much younger, maybe five or six, I'd go and sleep in my mam's bed if I'd had a nightmare. Pretty normal kid stuff, except I'd insist on holding one of her fingers. She'd ask if I could please instead just hold her hand because it was more comfortable for her, but I insisted. I remember how indomitably I believed it would provide the safest possible link to her in what seemed to me the likely event that someone would lean down and try and pull me away. I'd hold her finger so hard I'd be surprised if I didn't nearly snap it off, certainly restricting blood flow. But it felt so *safe*. A lingering pre-memory, perhaps, of tiny newborn fingers and fingernails curled around an enormous finger. I'd hold on for dear life.

I continued getting into bed next to my mam when I was scared until I was in secondary school. One night when I was sleeping in her bed with her, I woke up in the early hours and didn't feel scared any more. In fact, I couldn't remember why I'd felt fearful. So I tiptoed across the landing back to Liv's and my room, lifted the cover ready to get in my own bed *and someone was there*. I shit myself. Not literally, thank God, but it was one of the worst experiences of my existence. It soon became apparent why I'd no longer felt fearful, indeed was amnesiac about the root of it: Ashleigh was sleeping over (*duh*) and we were at that awkward age in growth terms that we couldn't really top and tail any more. I hadn't been scared in the first place. I was there in Mam's bed out of logistical necessity, too old now for finger-clutching. It was as though the years had been laid on top of one another like tracing paper and I'd muscle-memorised a short carpet-trodden route, best completed when half asleep and years younger, between the two parallel bedrooms. I was so shaken by the experience I had to crawl back in with my mam. *Ashleigh, I'm still your best friend, right? Could you just say it please?*

4
Beach

Our friend from primary school, Rose, had the world's most enviable magical house. To get to the house, you'd either come at it from behind and walk up a slightly sloping road, or else round the front, past a pub, and descend a ramp where the row of low houses stood. Before the tall wall that separated the row was a patch of grass with trees, and in the corner closest to the pub an unruly mess of brambles sat – though that seems too static a word to describe them. They were chaotic, dense, wild. We'd walk the thin wall, arms outstretched for balance, nervously giggling as we got close to the perilous corner. The laughs would turn smug as we passed it, but then when the wall came to an end we had to compose ourselves again to go back the way we came.

I think Rose's older sister had fallen in once. The horrifying thrill of the image, her falling while her long, wavy hair rushed up into the air above her, slower to react, made the wall-walk feel almost like a noble challenge, something out of CBBC's *Raven* – the brambles to be respected, revered. Sometimes, when we weren't skirting that scratchy mess of weeds, we'd scour the bricks for slugs and put them on our hands and arms. I remember when Rose put one on her face and we squealed, grossed out and fascinated by her boldness. I envied her intensely; she was so alive and carefree.

Walking into her house as a seven- or eight-year-old felt like walking into Aladdin's cave, my eyes twinkling with wonder no matter how many times we visited. It was a touch gloomy, I remember, and on the right-hand wall as you passed through the white wood-and-glass door was an array of gilded Venetian masks plucked from a fairy tale. They stared out from eyeless visages that always seemed to have a devilish smirk in them. Their brooding presence, suggestive of another world, entirely transfixed me. In the living room was a plain wooden piano, the sort we had in the main hall at primary school, a marvel to me and perhaps the inspiration for my accidental purchase of several pianos on Mam's eBay account once, for which she got banned. I'd wanted to learn to play so, so badly. Sometimes I'd sit on the comfy piano stool, my legs dangling, and stretch my tiptoes to reach the pedals. Rose taught me how to play 'Mary Had a Little Lamb', and I did, often. Even at so young an age, I was aching to understand myself, define myself. To find some activity that I could crawl into and find perfect shelter in, knowing it fit me snugly. If only I could find that *one* interest that I could point to and say 'That's who I am; that is my interest,' I'd somehow be whole, would have reconciled the shifting tectonic plates of myself like a jigsaw. In that illusion I saw certainty where around me, in me, there seemed to be none. It turns out the piano, no matter how much I wanted that to be *my thing*, wasn't after all. But the pull of Rose's piano, nevertheless, was almost supernaturally strong for me.

In the living room the 'arty' feel continued, with little panels of stained glass catching the light to the sound of wind chimes. The house had a beautiful eeriness that I couldn't and didn't want to shake. It felt like a doorway to a mysterious world, but one that went two ways and made me shiver. A liminal space, a space of freedom and possibility. The sisters had a dressing-up box – a great oak trunk is how I remember it. We'd gleefully dive into it, making ourselves look like hippies or witches, or just like adults: slapping our faces with make-up and wrapping strings of beads around our necks. Sometimes we'd stay over for tea and have tiny glasses of wine (juice) and what were to my mind unfathomably fancy meals. I remember having a spaghetti dish – it might have been carbonara – and in the middle of the table was a glass bowl of salad from which you were to serve yourself with 'tongs'. How civilised it seemed to me! Candles flickered in the room and I could feel their warmth.

The true treasure wasn't the seemingly bottomless dressing-up box, the wind chimes, the stained glass or even the masks or piano, however. It was the garden. It can't have been that big, just as the towering wall out front probably wasn't all that towering. But at the time it was a revelation. Where the only features in our garden were a step, a shed and The Dump, here there were swings, and a shed to dig holes behind. What drove our voracious urge to dig 'all the way to Australia' remains a mystery to me, though the unusual excitement at the thought of digging remains.

I was, am, drawn I think to the repetitive motion of digging: the rhythmic hi-ho of the seven dwarves; an axe raised with a whoosh and dropped with a thud; the Chuckle Brothers' 'to me, to you'. The precision of the focus, the utter mental and physical absorption in a task, enabled a sort of contained excitement that quieted my mind. An excitement that was rooted in the absolute present, with visible consequences.

We'd dig in Rose's garden on our hands and knees, co-conspirators with an array of tools pilfered from the shed and a little bucket of water beside us in case we needed to loosen up dry dirt for optimum excavation. Birds chirped; traffic whirred in the background. Occasionally we'd break our focus and strategise: 'Lauren, you take that wall there to make sure it doesn't collapse. Kitty, you push the mud pile away so it doesn't just fall back in.' It was a real operation and we performed it with the same kind of diligence and dedication you'd apply to a paid job for a big-shot client. We'd eventually hit clay, which became hard to shift, and as daylight waned we dropped tools to survey our work. Not all the way to Australia, OK, but up to my knee – I'd inevitably get into the hole – wasn't half bad either. Rose's mam would come round back to see what we'd been doing, and far from being angry she'd laugh her hearty, mellifluous laugh and say something like 'I'd been wondering what had been keeping yous quiet for so long!'

The world was ours to create. We climbed walls like they were cliff faces; dug in mud with the uncynical enthusiasm of kids expecting to strike gold first time; skirted thorns like if we fell we'd never stop, there'd be no bottom, we'd just land upright somewhere else.

What kid doesn't want at some point to be an archaeologist? To uncover buried cities and the secrets of the past? Trips to Whitby were common when we were little, and my fascination with discovery and earth most likely started there. Whale bones jutting out of the ground signalled the descent into the bustle of fudge stalls, olde sweet shops, fish and chip shops, and jewellery shops selling Whitby jet. There was a ruined abbey we'd see in the car on the way there; as we crested a hill, we saw it like a ship in the sea. We'd climb the torturous 199 steps to the church, scouring the graveyard for its oldest inhabitant. It was too dear to go into the abbey proper, but we didn't mind. The cold sea mist crawled up the cliff, and boat tours darted this way and that. From above, we watched screeching, hench seagulls swoop down, unafraid, onto tourists' chips. Outside some shops, centuries-old green glass bottles were sold individually. Fossils, too.

These were what I was most enamoured with. It feels prophetic or somehow meaningful that one of the UK's most prominent archaeologists and palaeontologists was called Mary Anning: a combination of my gran's name (Mary) and her sister's (Anne). In the early 1800s she found many, many fossils along the coast at Lyme Regis, including the first correctly identified ichthyosaur skeleton. She has one named after her: *Ichthyosaurus anningae*. And she almost joined them several times, like. On 19 August 1800, when Anning was just over a year old, she was being held by a neighbour called Elizabeth, who was standing with two other women under an elm tree watching a show being put on by a travelling company of horsemen, when lightning struck the tree, killing all three women – but not baby Mary. In 1833 she nearly perished in a landslide that killed her dog, Tray.

I shared her fascination with fossils and the earth with my gran Mary, and occasionally her sister Anne, who had the kind of house kids' dreams are made of: antique samurai swords mounted on the wall, objects picked up from her travels, a garden constantly revealing hidden ornamental treasures. Whenever we went to the Sunderland Museum and Winter Gardens with Gran, a short train or slightly longer bus journey away from Billingham, she'd let me get a new fossil or yet more fool's gold (I hoarded the stuff like the Golden Nuggets cereal prospector) from the gift shop before we departed. All the way home I'd cradle an ammonite in my palm, rubbing its surface, feeling the spiral of ancient time-worn grooves, a pleasurable sense of vertigo induced by touching something so many millions of years older than me. It grounded me somehow, made me feel a part of something big and important as my faith wavered. Though at this time I'd progressed from a Catholic primary school to a Catholic secondary school, I'd long started doubting the exciting stories of whales that swallowed men up whole and floods that wiped out species. At home we weren't very religious, so the weak hold these school-time stories had on my faith, if not my imagination, frayed slowly to snapping-point. So I couldn't believe in God, but I could believe in dinosaurs and the shit they left behind.

In Whitby the ammonites were ten times as big as my little specimens, which, for a time, I'd line up on my windowsill next to the smooth little bird skull I found in the garden. The window displays held big beefy ones that took my breath away. We'd walk over the stony beach desperately trying to find our own, however impressive, and I'd think of the elation of whoever first absent-mindedly overturned a rock with their boot only to discover it was no ordinary rock.

Whitby was somewhere my imagination could run wild and ragged and free. At Rose's, I felt the same. We'd jump around the furniture because the floor was lava. Freedom was ours and we grabbed it. We played hide-and-seek, and being scared of the dark I would crouch in a cupboard with my breaths becoming more rapid with every minute I wasn't found.

* * *

The older I've got, the more I've realised hard work and suffering don't immediately mean success. The A to B equation got a little more complicated. Liv and I were always the smartest at school, or rather we were picked out as top of the class early on and therefore cultivated at the expense of other, struggling students. In any case, as it was, our school reports glowed, and as we sat in front of a teacher who was probably no older than we are now, we'd bask in the warm praise flowing over us while Mam and Dad – and then later just Mam or Dad – exuded pride. It was addictive. And easy. We'd try hard to be well behaved and to absorb as much information as possible.

I loved school and the attendant attention, as this story will hopefully show (Punch and Judy curtains open wide, to fanfare, in the dark belly of Billingham town centre, where kids sit on the concrete). One night we'd had the treat of staying at my Aunty Jojo and Uncle Andy's – this was my Mam's sister and her husband. They didn't yet have children whose attention we could be fiercely jealous of, and we'd sat on their big leather sofa with a bowl of Minstrels watching movies, our little legs straight and poking off the edge, toes out the end of a blanket. They spoiled us, taking us often in their little silver car to Metroland at the Metrocentre in Gateshead.

For the uninitiated, the fairground opened in 1988, and it looked like it. Were it still open, the producers of *Stranger Things* would be all over it, so alike in aesthetic was it to that shopping centre where they fight the Demogorgon at the end of series three. It would have provided an amazing backdrop to a thriller, but perhaps that applies to all spaces created for children, with their nightmarish creatures with perennial smiles that barely conceal the *things they've seen*. (There's a thirteen-year difference between us and my little sister – Dad's and Ruth's little girl, Lucy – and watching CBeebies when you're a bit older is nothing short of a bad trip.) Speaking of nightmares, in 2003 some 19 children aged between 9 and 11 had to be rescued by firefighters using cherry pickers when they were left trapped on the Metroland roller coaster. A mechanical failure left them suspended above the ground. According to the marketing executive, whatever that is, in a news story at the time, '… the train was not able to get up the incline and it rolled backwards'. I can't help but wonder: for how many of those kids was it their first go? Did their shrieks immediately change to genuine fear? Did they think it was part of the ride? Or could they read on the seasoned kids' faces that no, it wasn't. Nobody was hurt, so maybe they tugged on their mothers' sleeves next Saturday to please, please go back.

Metroland was the largest indoor theme park in Europe, the jewel in the north's crown. But in April 2008, when I was 12, it closed. Four thousand people signed a petition to prevent the closure, but it was no use. After a final weekend, 'The Last Ride Weekend', where tickets were £5 for an entire day (an entire day!), that fantastic, unlikely hall of screams fell silent.

I wish I had adequate words to describe this festival of colour and sound and light, cartoon faces and swinging chairs, squealing kids and competing music. Imagine that the sweetest, stickiest candyfloss became a place. Nestled oddly in the enormous shopping centre, it felt a world unto itself. Rising impossibly high from the ground up was a 'Chairoplane' that flung gleeful tiny bodies with socked feet above our heads. The waltzers that would painfully fling your neck back, preventing you from being able to lift your head: a terrifying, exhilarating prospect. A small Ferris wheel, whose pastel-coloured elephant-shaped cars bore only a metal bar across a foot-long gap to keep you from plummeting to the floor. That, and our own impulse not to do so. I tried not to think about it.

The roller coaster was the pièce de résistance. Our thin wrists adorned with a wristband smugly declaring 'Day Pass', we felt like sickly VIPs as we jumped out and scrambled up the stairs ready for another go. A clock face that was *actually* a plump pink face, reminiscent of *Thomas & Friends*, ticked away the precious hours. I can still smell the warm scent of cheap American-style hotdogs and cherry pop.

I read that after it closed, the roller coaster – *the* roller coaster – was moved to The Big Sheep (which I like to think is a homage to Raymond Chandler), a farm-themed amusement park in Devon, which for a few years let people from the North East ride for free. I imagine a dad, let's call him Gary, Gaz, being reunited with the coaster as though it were an old steed he'd been fond of as a youth, smiling a half-smile as he pats it fondly on its curved side. Big 'that'll do pig, that'll do' energy. I'm sure we first watched the film, *Babe* that is, at Jojo and Andy's.

Perhaps we'd been with them to Metroland on a Sunday – I recall it was either only open on a weekend (which makes sense, given, you know, school) or that it was cheaper – and that's why Jojo was dropping us off at the school gates that day instead of us taking our usual three-minute walk round the corner. I recall no other time she took us to school, so this must've been the scenario. She stepped out of the three-door car to lower the driver's seat and let me out, and as I barrelled out after Liv, my frilly-socked black shoe got looped in the seatbelt, the metal buckle scratching the grey pavement like nails on a chalkboard, and I slammed face-first to the floor. It wasn't my first injury, mind – far from it.

Aged 3, Liv and I had been at Grandma and Grandad Maureen's (he's called Gordon, but she was called Maureen and that's what we called them), dancing to the *Postman Pat* music (apparently my family just couldn't get enough of Royal Mail). We were seeing who could spin the fastest and I twirled head-first into the marble hearth and cracked my head open. I won, but at what cost? At what cost? My uncle Chris took me to the hospital, carrying me bleeding profusely into A & E. So much blood in such a tiny head. I wasn't bothered by the blood, though. In fact, all I could think about was that I was outside without shoes on, which was against the rules. Once I'd reluctantly been sewn up and a couple of weeks had passed, I was left with a gnarly scar on my forehead that's there, if I frown, even now. Sat at the table with our prison-like primary-coloured dinner trays at Holy Rosary, I'd pretend to the other kids I was in psychic commune with Harry Potter, who'd occupy any empty seat at our table as we scooped bricks of Victoria sponge with pink custard into our sloppy gobs.

This time, the time outside the playground, wasn't quite as dramatic as *Postman Pat*-gate. But I was. I bawled my eyes out as an egg-shaped bump took over my fore-head and Liv looked on in horror. I wouldn't be going to school today. But there behind the pain was a nagging worry that I was going to fall behind by missing today's six hours, a nagging worry that's stretched far into adult-hood and worker-hood, and pinches and pulls at my brain whenever I take a day off.

Liv and I were reading well above our 'reading age', whatever the fuck that means (but we liked the sound of it) as early as Year 3, and from there we were bumped into different classes for numeracy. As a Year 4 sat at a diddy round table with Year 5s, it was intimidating and they sensed it, playing with me about things I was too young to understand and giggling among themselves when I faltered. After one such instance, I arrived home – pausing to collect a Babybel and some ham from the fridge to devour in front of *Arthur* or *Watch My Chops* – and asked Mam, casually, what a penis was.

* * *

There's something of this institutionalised levelling-up beneath my childhood love for digging holes in the ground, I think, and perhaps a clue to why I eventually started excavating my skin. 'A' leads quite simply to 'B': dig hard enough and you'd get a hole, job done. It wasn't always about finding treasure. It was about digging a hole for the sake of digging a hole. The hole was the endgame, and I knew how to do it well. I receive recognition from those in positions to weave their fingers together and give me a foothold as I climb, and it spurs me on; I do well in the exams; repeat. You don't think about where you might be climbing to. It doesn't matter because the world is yours to comprehend.

Only later would the concept of 'productivity' enter my mind and whisper 'What's the point? You don't know if you'll find anything.' Now it's not enough to just see what you *might* find – I need some guarantee that this is going to be a worthwhile use of my time, that it's going to advance me somehow. And that can stop you digging in the spot where the chunky fossils are. I hate that it's taken me so long to truly appreciate the live laugh love phrase, *it's not the destination but the journey that counts*, not least because it was likely written in cursive on every cushion lining the shelves of the town square's B&M and then my mam's house, but there we are.

Throughout my life, punctuating the endless drone of anxiety fizzing like static between background and foreground, I've experienced these odd moments of piercing calm that I think of as that 'you are the world' feeling. Holding a fossil, feeling Whitby's chill sea breeze whip my face, or touching the bark of an ancient tree bring it on, but unreliably. You can't *try* to have it, I've found. Just like you can't really 'try to relax'. What kind of phrase is that? The first time I remember feeling momentarily aglow with centredness and beingness was in Mam's car on the ramp leading off the A19 onto the roundabout in Norton that can take you across the motorway into Billingham, of all places. Out of nowhere, I looked out of the window at the leafy bushes to my left and was struck by calm, like sun-lit water tumbling over mossy rocks. I must have been 10 or 11. The feeling was gone in an instant, but the warmth stayed with me, in me, like a seed in my belly that made me feel alive, and which I knew would be there no matter what. In times of adversity or stress, the light will occasionally break through and momentarily illuminate the gloom, and I feel the seed. It comes most frequently, too, among really old buildings, like churches.

I know, I know, I sound like a dick. But in those moments it's like I can feel history, feel the layers and layers of family never known to me. I feel the church, hear its bells ringing like they have done for hundreds of years, and I can breathe like it's the first time. I think my 'you are the world' feeling is being completely in the moment and also feeling timeless, rendering the word 'moment' as insubstantial as the wind. It lets me shake off my own history for an instant, to be a living breathing animal on whom there's no pressure to be anything but what it is; my only sense of crooked spirituality lies in this. I explain it to myself as being like God: *God lies in those moments*, I think, but it isn't anything like an anachronistically white man with a beard making earthquakes and shit happen. It's sort of a glimpse of life from the outside. A sun-broken cloud, the perspective of the rain. Being outside of yourself, outside of time, taking a break from yourself for one tiny, everything moment. The time spent digging a hole or climbing a gnarled tree until you're hungry. Kids have it, without realising it, this freedom from the constraints of time. Innocence, I guess some might call it.

Utter abandon – taking the not-knowingness of inno-cence to its furthest possible conclusion, right to the other end of the spectrum – seems in many ways a logical continuation of the idea of innocence, even if it does end in its opposite. The ancient Greeks were all about losing themselves in Dionysian frenzies of debauchery. During our Year 10 house parties, drinking Apple Sourz and snogging each other (and throwing up neon green liquid before resuming the snogging), I'd say we got pretty close to bacchanalia. For those who entirely reasonably are unaware of the meanings behind every other word I've just said, let me take a moment to clarify a couple of things before we continue:

1. Sourz is a 15 per cent-strength alcoholic beverage best served, regardless of the bottle's 'serving suggestion', neat and, apparently, slightly warm. It also came in a range of flavours – cherry was another favourite – including ones that had *milk* in them, like strawberries and cream. You had to drink these ones all in the same night (which we also did with the non-perishables) because they did not age well left in the cupboard. No siree. Learnt that the hard way.

2. Dionysus was the Greek god best associated with wild and ecstatic religious rites, also known as bacchanalia. In later traditions he became associated with wine and the loss of inhibition. See? Sourz. A bacchanalian – also known as a Dionysian – party is a wild night out, essentially. The night out to end all nights out, like your best friend's 21st. It feels appropriate that there's a pub in Newcastle, home of trebles and ten-inch heels, called The Bacchus. The idea is tied up with the idea of the self, and the paradoxical live-laugh-love-y notion that you have to lose yourself to find yourself. It's the idea that only by casting off the shackles of the self, its wants and insecurities and foibles, can we truly experience the fullness of being and reveal our creative, peace-loving selves, man.

* * *

Such a dispensation of identity, the drop becoming the wide-open universal ocean free to flow, subjective giving way to objective, has of course a darker, dangerous side. Without our civilised sense of humanity, the moral and societal norms that ostensibly keep polite society ticking away, we'd all be feral and unpredictable (Aristotle thought that going to the theatre would get all this wild instinct out of our systems so the world could stay as it was). Sounds pretty sexy, hey? Well, orgies are part and parcel of the idea of the Dionysian, but so is murder, destruction, inhumanity. That's what happens to the students in Donna Tartt's *The Secret History*, who, having become fascinated with the Greeks, performed frequent rituals that brought them out of the mundanity of their lives but ended up leading them to commit a heinous crime. In Athenian playwright Euripides' play *The Bacchae*, the women of Thebes in a Dionysian rite tear a man literally limb from limb under the devilish god's intoxicating influence.

You'll be pleased to know that I haven't torn any man limb from limb, though I've been sorely tempted. But I do crave the escape from my thoughts, from myself, these mad feral orgiastic parties seem to offer. The Ibiza boat tours marketing people really ought to lead with that, honestly.

My way of numbing myself, of momentarily slipping out of my mind, has for whatever reason taken the form of skin picking. I damage only myself. But is it the same as the Dionysian feeling of utter escape I've described, this absence of self? I'm not sure.

Lauren Brown

For starters I'm far too anxious not to worry that I won't find my way back to myself again, since losing yourself completely seems kind of the deal. I'd still be holding a finger to make sure if I was taken away I'd wake myself up. There's no way I could lose myself to picking entirely; I haven't let myself. I've been tempted to just let go, to pick ad infinitum and completely disfigure myself. But even though it's got to the point that it could very well threaten my way of life – stopping me going outside and socialising, making me a recluse – I've always had one foot in. I can't help it. That belly-seed doesn't want me to lose myself, no matter how much relief it might bring. I know behind the numbness there's no ecstasy, no heightened sense of beingness in the lack of beingness, instead just a vacuum.

If the numbing of myself by picking has been my crack of the Dionysian whip, I'm not 21 any more – I can't keep it up. I think of my 'picking sessions' – belly lumped over the white lip of the sink to get as close as possible, never close enough, to my face – as a 'frenzy' on very bad days. But I don't want to spin uncontrollably through life any more, someone who tears their skin apart as though trying to escape it.

I want the peace and quiet and security of not losing myself to paradoxically find myself, but to be very much myself and to be OK with that. Maybe that's the 'of this world' feeling. I don't want extremes any more; I don't want all or nothing; I want to accept the existence of both. I don't want to escape any more, into my numb, picking void; I want to feel it all. But life has always just felt so very, very loud.

I may very well be overthinking this. It has been known. So let me just say, Sourz and snogs aside, that I think I need to stop trying so hard to escape and instead start inhabiting the present moment, no matter how roaring loud it feels. Without the self-preservation tactic I thought was shielding me from pain. Hands, I know you think what you've been doing has been helping. It makes me feel oddly sad when I think about this, but it seems to me that my mind, my hands, have been engaged in a misguided attempt to look after me, not destroy me. But that's exactly what they've paradoxically been doing.

Seaton Carew beach is, I've come to realise, one of the places where I have encountered this 'of the world' feeling most often. Here, my self-narrated preoccupation with the world and how I'm experiencing it moment to moment slips away; I step out of the way of myself, and I experience life, for however brief an interlude, unmediated.

It's not a place that's all golden sand and crystalline waves, though, Seaton – make no mistake about that. I remember in 2007 when the place was dubbed Seaton Canoe after one John Darwin was found to have faked his own death in a 'canoe accident' there. Presumed dead, he'd actually been living it up in Panama before coming home to live in a bedsit next door to his former home on the seafront. While he was away he used the name John

Jones, disturbingly that of a baby who'd died in Sunderland in 1950. My cul-de-sac was a street of *Coronation Street*-watching curtain twitchers avid for the scandal its inhabitants so often provided. Mam was mad for it, a shadow behind the blinds watching and tutting and 'ee'ing as silent but flashing police cars and ambulances pulled into the street in the early hours. And well, what a story Seaton Canoe was. A faked death, forged passports, scandal, intrigue. Watching the coverage as a 12-year-old was riveting and disquieting. Also of urgent national concern that same year, 2007, was the frantic and constant coverage of Madeleine McCann's disappearance. Holding on to Mam's finger didn't seem quite so outrageous, then.

When you see your mam cry for the first time, really cry, it shatters irreparably the childhood delusion – exposes it as just that – that the adults know what they're doing and are in control. That myth is wiped away and the world encroaches, seeping like noxious gas from 'out there' to 'in here'. I was at that age when my boobs were coming in in earnest, when I began noticing myself as a body in the eyes of boys and men, and what little security I felt we had was being undermined by the constant cycle of intense news that filled up the lamp-lit living room each evening. The rules of the world as we'd been taught them were crumbling; people did bad things, and I simply could not look away. I was darkly dazzled by this other, shadowy world that had, unknown to me, been existing alongside my own all this time, just behind the curtain.

At the time all this was happening, our living room rug was spilt with glossy real-life magazines proclaiming from bombastic covers even more outrageous stories of murder, betrayal and botched surgery. 'My Husband Thinks He's a Fray Bentos Pie' here, 'I Sold My Son for a Bag of Chips' there. I'd lie on my tummy flicking through them, the *Sun* and the Sunday supplements. A favourite game of mine and Liv's was the 'that or that?' game, where we'd go through them all front-to-back and speedily choose between the things on the page. *That or that? That. That or that? That. That or that? That.* We'd read our horoscope together and wonder whether it was true that our love lives really were going to take a saucy twist this week. Unlikely at St Michael's, in Year 8, but there you go.

Pumped up, then, on *EastEnders* (Stacey and Bradley, never forget) and tabloids, the fact that Real Life was happening in my real life was quite simply exhilarating. It gave me a taste, too, for the macabre, in a way that was palatable. Close enough to home, but not too close as to be actually scary. As someone whose mind lived on the precipice of constant, unshakeable doom, being able to fall but not really fall was, I suppose, akin to knocking the glass of coke over just to get it out of the way. *Schadenfreude* is often spoken of only in terms of the enjoyment at watching someone fall, for example, but there's a darker truth buried therein that underscores horror movies and true crime.

It did get too close to home sometimes, though; the shadows were never really very far away. My mam's cousin, for example, was stabbed to death in her bed by her copper husband when Liv and I were nine because he'd found out she was going to leave him. We were too young to be told that her kids were the ones who found her; maybe we overheard it, but we knew. Then there was the case of 22-year-old Julie Hogg who was found stuffed underneath a boarded-up bathtub in Billingham, in 1989. Way before my time, but the story was something that haunted me as a kid even more than the bogeyman tales that wafted into the local kids' collective consciousness. Local lore. And then something happened on Seaton Carew beach, too. Not to somebody decades ago, or even to a parent's cousin who I'd never met, but to someone who'd combed my hair and plaited it and who'd seemed like a good person but maybe wasn't.

My mam had been friends with her, let's call her Kate, for a couple of years. She was the girlfriend of an acquaintance. She had dyed-blonde hair and a voice croaky from smoking, but was tanned and youthful with a wicked cackle of a laugh and always treats in her bag for the kids. Kate had a daughter younger than Liv and me, about six, who we played with and doted on. Her hair was naturally blonde. When I look back, it's obvious now Kate was troubled, like Mam. Maybe that's what brought them so close. They'd sit and drink together, and once, my mam being the deeply giving person she is, told Kate, after Kate had complimented her shoes, that if she liked them she could have them if she wanted. I remember next standing peeking around the corner of Mam's bedroom door frame while Kate proceeded to ransack Mam's wardrobe for shoeboxes that were then hastily ferried to her car.

In 2007 Kate killed herself on Seaton beach. The beach where we'd pitched a tent, roasted marshmallows and barbecued, where we'd paddled in icy water that would make us shriek as it reached our white pot bellies. She had drunk a lot and taken a lot of tablets; they were lying next to her. Her body was found by a man walking his dog one morning. She'd apparently sent a flurry of text messages and calls to a friend that night. She was 34 and had in her hand a picture of her daughter. I can't remember ever seeing her daughter again after that.

We'd been to Seaton Carew with Kate before, going to a little bay round the side I've never been back to since. The day was long, so long, and we drank up every last drop of it. A ramshackle tent was packed in the car and put up beside a wind-breaking dune whose rushes swayed like air-whipped hair. We hunkered down until the sun set and the glow of firelight was increasingly all we could see. That, and the twinkling many-coloured lights emanating from the intricate frame of the steelworks that are as much a feature of the Teesside skyline as the stars. Like Miyazaki's clanking, tin-banging *Howl's Moving Castle*, disused oil rigs add to the ruinous cityscape like metallic plants pulled up hard from the roots. As you drive by, you can see the parts that were below the water's surface, rusted and fraying, the scrapyards a not-quite ghost town whose spectral flames illuminate a rat race of meandering, endless tubes. Grey chimneys pump out great billowing plumes that disappear into the white sky like the pipes of the men who'd clock off and go down the working men's club for a smoke and some darts.

It seems so unmanned now, despite all appearances still chugging away, still flame-lit and bright on the horizon. From the distance of the beach it's impossible to see any people, but on the drive past the gull-swarmed rubbish tip towards Seaton you can occasionally spot men in hard hats, and a security barrier letting cars in and out. But it's infrequent, and to me it seems as abandoned as the swathe of old pacer train carriages lining the abandoned tracks near Middlesbrough that you can see from the A19 fly-over, or the half-sunken asbestos-filled boat still moored in Middlesbrough's dockyard where my mam's dad, Joseph, apparently used to work.

Grandma and Grandad Maureen met when they were both working at the ICI. Each looked like a Hollywood movie star. In one black-and-white photograph shown to me by my Grandad, he's 18, shirtless, and hanging off the side of a sailing boat. He was in the army, then, travelling around Asia, and in the picture he's overexposed by bright sunshine and absolutely beaming. They each had a very different temperament, my grandma and grandad, but it worked. My grandma was boisterous and loud, bolshy and unafraid to be forward. I have a hazy memory of her telling me that when she saw my grandad from a walk-way above, looking down at her, she said something to

the effect of 'Well there's no use just standing there looking. Aren't you going to talk to me?' He's very shy, my
grandad, quiet, was happy to let her wild, irresistible
personality take centre stage. When she was really ill, the
dementia taking root, she'd think they were young again
and would flirt so shamelessly with him at family gather-
ings she'd make him blush. She had an incredible set of
pipes on her and sang all day every day. She was one to
be heard, alright. They used to go dancing in
Middlesbrough, she no doubt dragging '*my* Mr Brown'
reluctantly onto the dance floor or crooning wickedly at
him as he's nudged in the ribs by teasing mates. Apparently,
she sang on stage sometimes. Back in those days you
could walk up the many, many steps of the Transporter
Bridge to a nauseatingly high gangway that linked
Billingham to Middlesbrough across the Tees, so they'd
stumble home either along the quiet A19 or over there. It
had to be closed eventually because people would drunk-
enly fall off, or sometimes jump. You can do bungee
jumps off it now.

I can still hear my grandma singing 'Do-Re-Mi'. She
loved *The Sound of Music*. Once, in Berlin, my friends
and I went for tea at this wartime dance hall strung with
big fat fairy lights. The weather was temperate, so we ate
outside (I had a beige soup that was surprisingly good for
something so bland looking) and when the boys went off
we three girls went excitedly inside. I thought of her
immediately. She'd not yet passed away; it was just that
the space reminded me so much of her I felt I could see

her, young, twirling completely freely on the wooden dance floor in an A-line dress making perfect circles as she moved. With dance-hall-cum-bingo-hall vibes, it had glitzy red and gold streamers pouring down the walls and people of all ages danced together. Heads pressed to life-partners' chests, kids stomping and spinning and running, young Berliners, us.

Now she's gone. My grandad lives alone in the bunga-low where they spent their last years together, scared to come outside even for a socially distanced walk, no doubt eating the chopped pork and lettuce sandwiches he used to make us in that little kitchen out the back when she was still here.

The decrepitude of Seaton Carew, Seaton Canoe; its dated art deco architecture; glorious summers spent unselfcon-sciously stripping down in blinding sunlight; the semi-abandoned aura of the distant steelworks; Kate; her daughter; the way the wet sand reflects the sky so perfectly it feels like walking through heaven; the treks up and down the dunes, getting further and further away from the car – all of it makes up the haunting splendour of the place. The laid-bare history of an empty kids' paddling pool, fairground rides covered with waterproof sheets. You'd think they'd been left there, that the pool wouldn't ever have lukewarm water in it again. But then you'd return and, like a clock that had been wound back to a minute before midnight, the place was alive with toddlers held by the armpits, spreading who knows what grim infant disease into the water, and the smell of cheap burgers next to a ticket booth. (My favourite food stall, which remains shuttered there, simply offers 'pork' as one of its advertised options.) The next time you returned, it would be still again, as though the chatter and action and fairground rides had all been a ghostly mirage.

The bus station, flanking the white art deco clock, felt Victorian. Maybe I'd been influenced at this time by a school trip, chaperoned as always by Grandma Mary, to a museum where we'd been allowed to dress up in Victorian garb, but as we sat and ate fish and chips on those wooden benches, I could see ladies of the promenade holding their parasols in one hand while urging littl'uns to 'mind your ice cream doesn't drip on your nice clothes'. I don't remember ever seeing any actual buses go by or stop at the station.

You could feel history in the air, so nearly see it exactly as it once was: every beach-side B&B sign as bright as the day it was freshly painted and bursting with guests ready to head out tomorrow to secure a decent chalet. I can remember being inside one of those multicoloured chalets, now gone: a mere wooden hut with a bench, the smell of damp salty wood, chattering teeth and feet swinging. They were nothing, but to a kid they were a brand-new house with a driveway and gated entrance.

Seaton was one of the locations Dad would take me, Liv, and our cousin Aidan to on days out. Being a year older and a boy almost as boisterous as I was, I'd follow Aidan to the ends of the earth, doing whatever cheeky thing he was doing, be that splashing in brown puddles, launching ourselves into piles of autumn leaves or racing to the top of the playground climbing thingy. The thingy was a vast matrix of interlocking blue rope in a diamond shape; you climbed on and into this thing and got swallowed up by its maze of endless footholds. And there were two of them, two azure ziggurats connected by a wibbly-wobbly bridge made from the same thick, scratchy rope and wooden planks. Climbing to the top sorted the wheat from the chaff, and my body flew up there faster than my mind, such that I'd occasionally have to whine to Dad to lift me down. But the best fun wasn't to be found in the playgrounds but among the trees. Regardless of the weather, we'd wrap up on Sundays and go for a walk in the woods or a park.

It had to be on Sundays because Saturdays were for the cricket – which all the postie men in my family for some reason love, despite it being objectively the most mind-numbingly boring 'sport' I've ever not watched. Us kids would go and 'watch' (read: run around the edges of the pitch, weaving behind the umpire's box, etc.) occasionally, mainly for the miniature bar/tuckshop inside what might loosely be called a 'clubhouse' (in reality a stinky green Portakabin). There, we'd be allowed 20p for a gummy snake that would be pulled out of the plastic box that sat on the bar by the till.

So we're at the park, and I *idolise* Aidan. I always have, as an aside, and it's not because he was two school years ahead of us, even though that alone would've done it. It's not even because he once told a teacher to 'fuck off', something I would never have dared to do. It's because he's an insanely smart person and devilishly funny. We'd sit at his computer as kids looking at memes and funny comic strips for hours on end. He reassured me when I started at secondary school and started having dissociative spells where, during lessons, my brain would become weirdly tingly and everything would go really, really quiet and suddenly really, really slow. I still don't know though what the heck that was all about. He was the only person I told, but he got it.

These trips to the park, they were before computers and memes and dissociative episodes, when our small bodies were swamped by waterproof bomber jackets and welly boots and we were excited by big piles of leaves. Aidan would rush through them unthinkingly, miles in front of fast-walking Dad, throwing himself through and over them, sweeping armfuls of them into the air to fall down on our ecstatically giggling heads. Everything he did seemed hilarious and marvellous and daring, and Liv and I trailed behind him like groupies as he bolted between trees and retrieved long, damp sticks as tall as we were. If he decided to test the depth of a wide, muddy bog by plunging knee-deep into it, I devotedly followed, once getting stuck and slowly falling face-first into the mud after forgetting I was shorter in stature than him. I imagine he gave me a solemn nod after an annoyed Dad had angrily pulled me from this fast-slurping quicksand, like I was Aidan's apprentice and I'd passed a test.

Sometimes at the park, depending on which one we went to, we'd muster the courage to walk up to and feed the huge cows that were behind a wooden fence. Aidan once rushed eagerly forward, suddenly unafraid of the hungry beasts, to feed them some grass he grabbed from the ground below. Inspired by Aidan's boldness, I decided to toddle up behind him to have a go at feeding them myself. I copied his actions entirely, but accidentally picked up a fistful of stinging nettles.

Despite that experience, even now, as I walk through nature reserves or down streets, I absentmindedly, compulsively rip unseen leaves of trees to shred with my fingers before plucking more from whichever shrubbery I pass. More than once have I been accidentally pricked, thrust into a sudden consciousness of what I was doing. Like the irresistible beer mats or paper menus of whatever pub I go to, I'll look down only to realise I've completely decimated whatever was in my vicinity to decimate. Maybe Liv or a friend will have snapped me out of the accompanying daze, telling me to stop it. A hand plunged into a coat not worn for some time will occasionally hit upon a shredded leaf from last year's winter or a mangled receipt that stood no chance.

The beach, even with bulging dark grey clouds threatening imminent rain, was perhaps a more favourable location, then, for a dad who needed to be able to keep his eye on three kids full of beans and giddy from each other's company. Somewhere where there were no thick wooded areas for us to cause unseen mischief among. As in Rose's garden, our primary objective at Seaton was clear: dig. For as long and as deep as possible. The hours slipped by as unnoticed as air as we scooped out great handfuls of increasingly wet sand, packed the walls until they were rock solid, excavated big stones that jutted out of them, flicked aside deep-buried shells and finally climbed one after the other into what we had done. We were inside the beach and it was inside us, wind-whipped sand lacing our hair and crunching between our teeth, filling our shoes and crusting our fingernails. We became a part of the landscape instead of observers of it, not set apart but a part of nature.

I think about this sometimes when I walk through Cambridge. It takes a conscious and strained effort for me not to put on a podcast I won't really follow to drown out the world and to get the walk over with as soon as possible. But I'm getting better at it. I look at the wild fen cows and how brilliantly and unapologetically cowish they are. They're not wondering whether or not they're acting enough like a cow. They don't think, or at least I assume they don't think, about what the hell they're doing with their lives. As far as I can see they're just happy to have grass to munch on. They're just being cows.

I'm trying harder to just be a cow. To feel like an animal in the most evolutionary sense of the word as often as I can. On the days I go for a walk, even a little one, I catch glimpses of that 'of the world' feeling and feel as much a part of my surroundings as the sky and the trees and the birds, feeling both unimportant and yet everything. I wonder whether those fen cows see people walking past and acknowledge us. I wonder whether the seagulls screeching overhead at Seaton thought, 'Huh, look, some young humans,' or just thoughtlessly, miraculously accepted us.

In bed after a knackering day of hardcore digging, I'd imagine the sea's edge creeping closer and closer to our hole. We'd strategically set it back to avoid it being filled too fast, but whether we said it or not we knew it would almost definitely be filled with water, whether deep in the night or sooner. As our stomachs rumbled and we edged towards the end of our dig, we'd see and feel it getting closer, perhaps looking up after minutes, hours of unbroken focus to see the world had shifted, or just knowing inherently that as the day grew dark the water came. I didn't mind that the hole wouldn't last, it didn't matter. There was always next time, and next time we'd dig even deeper.

5
Nails

Sitting up as straight as humanly possible was the only way I could see of securing the best instruments from the Holy Rosary instruments trolley, which was wheeled out every Wednesday Assembly. Wednesday Assembly was for singing songs in praise of Jesus and, occasionally, if we were lucky, a song that instead involved us chanting 'Gimme one, gimme two, gimme one, two, three, four' followed by (sung) 'We are the children of [insert school name]!' (Holy Rosary School was three syllables out and quite a mouthful). At least, sitting as bolt upright as humanly possible was the tactic we had all settled on as most likely to be conducive to success, more than a handful of us having no doubt through experience deduced the inefficacy of begging and/or crying.

Rows and rows of tiny bodies, the younger half of the primary school, sat attentively, not out of any reverence or existential understanding of the biblical overtones of the sessions – though they did include some cool stories about a superhero and his mates – but because the real draw was that little metal trolley that jangled with bells as it was rolled, nay, *glided*, across the smooth wooden floor of the hall to the front. There, an enormous wooden pole topped with a brassy hook was used by the cheerful music teacher, mumbling as she manoeuvred it (arm stretched high; she was short) to pull down a white screen hitherto rolled up to the ceiling. Once in position, the projector – which sat square in the middle of the front row, obstructing at least one or two little pairs of eyes – was switched on and lyrics would appear beamed onto the screen. Sometimes they were handwritten, and the teacher's hand as she tried to perfectly straighten the transparent sheet would cast huge black shadows on the wall and screen.

Disappointingly, the first few numbers were usually only accompanied by the piano, but some of the songs were such bangers that I didn't mind waiting: 'Walk, walk in the light' and 'Follow me, follow me, leave your home and family' (always felt that one was asking a bit much). Looking like you weren't overly bothered about the trolley made it more likely you'd get something good off it, so faux ambivalence was the name of the game: turning 180 degrees around to look at the blue, cracked, plasticky PE mats stacked like pancakes, the many-sized hobby horses and long wooden benches amidst which the trolley was nestled, would, we imagined, dampen our chances.

Oh yes, I knew the game, alright. No wriggly bottom, no surreptitious twizzles of the waist to glance over your shoulder: the complete physical quelling of any signs of impatience or irritability. Eyes front, mouth a wide deferential 'O'. And anyway, if we were good, some of the songs would include clapping and ('Sing Hosanna!') rhythmic banging on the dusty old floor.

The atmosphere would change after we'd sung a few songs. We collectively sensed that the teacher, whether by softly closing the lid of the piano or simply shifting slightly in posture, probably relishing her sudden cult-leader-like power, was about to unveil the trolley – as though it were a brand-new car she was modelling on a rotating platform. All thirty or so of us were suddenly the alien plushies from *Toy Story*, marvelling at 'the claaaaw' as if we hadn't, you know, lived beneath it this entire time. Sit up straight, she'd say, and here is where I, forgive the boast, *absolutely shone*. I'd stretch my torso as tall as my crossed legs would allow, raising my chin to the sky for maximum impact, and tuck my crossed arms with hunched shoulders as close to my face as possible. It probably looked like I was either having some kind of seizure, participating in a gurning contest, or trying to struggle out of a straitjacket (which would've probably genuinely benefited both myself and those poor bastards burdened with my care).

Everyone did it, the floor suddenly a sea of pleading eyes and desperate bodies begging for anything, please merciful and beneficent God, *anything*, but the triangle. The polite tinkling triangle, whose soft and ringing reverberations though very lovely ultimately did absolutely nada for a kid who wanted to create as much green-lighted din as humanly possible before the clock struck 11 (it was already edging on ten to, according to the analogue clock on the wall; time was of the essence).

After an interminable wait the gavel eventually dropped and the kids chosen to pick something from the trolley today would walk smugly over to it, plucking jingling tambourines from the top basket while their comrades wished death on them and their families. Tambourines looted fast, the next row of lucky pupils would rush ('one at a time, and slowly please') to the scraps like ravenous hyenas, the lucky few at the front of the queue grabbing the second most-coveted item: that scrapy fish thing. Oh, it was a thing of beauty, that fish block, painted colourfully in a way vaguely reminiscent of Marcus Pfister's book *The Rainbow Fish*, a copy or two of which likely awaited us back in the classroom. The fish block had several functions: you could smack it hard with its complementary wooden stick or scrape its ribbed tummy (which I imagined were it alive it would enjoy like a dog). I liked this particular function very much, enjoyed the vibrations on my fingertips as I glided across those bumpy canyons, their song transferring through my stick and into my hands.

I didn't know at the time, nor do I think any of the teachers knew (if they did, they didn't tell us) that this instrument wasn't officially called a 'scrapy fish thing' but a 'guiro'. Traditionally played by Latin American singers like the maracas (not much further down our pecking order), they weren't always in the shape of a fish. Some, I've since seen, are squat and round and deeply coloured like aubergines, others more like parched sweet potatoes or small fibreglass missiles.

Once all the tier-one instruments had been claimed, a fair amount of smugness, albeit lesser, still emanated from the last row of kids lucky enough to have been chosen this time round as Guardians of the Trolley Instruments. Between them, they cleaned the cart's metal ribs of meat: many-belled bell trees whose fat baubles looked like fruit; drums without the embellishment of tambourines, all *tambour* and no *ine*; and the regrettable triangle that rejected the grasping fists of energetic children by refusing to sound if not handled with care.

I looked forward to the sessions with a mixture of trepidation and excitement every week, and this one was no different. There was nothing notable about the way I sat down that day, my tights as usual making my bum itchy from long contact with the floor, carefully shifting my weight every now and then to prevent it from going numb, the twin tops of my sitting bones pointing sharp and uncomfortable into the hard floor so as to prevent volunteering myself as a wriggler. Sure, this stuff made me pretty anxious sometimes, and hyper-aware that sometimes my overheating mind and urge to move would deprive me of my chance of tambourine glory. But this internal war was silent, broken only by occasional fidgeting and sweaty palms: I blended in with the blue-jumpered crowd.

Changes of mood gathered as suddenly as storm clouds in me even then, and that day clear skies blended into swelling grey with a rapidity new even to me. Perhaps I'd been biting my nails and that's why I was suddenly, veins iced, stopped short by what I saw before me.

My fingers have always been a site of relentless destruction. My ability to find something to latch my tiny teeth onto despite the desolate and empty landscape their bleeding, painful prey presented, must have, now I look at it, laid the foundation for the excoriating habit that erupted decades later. I haven't stopped biting my nails, by the way. I've had spells of success but have always been drawn back downwards in the end.

Then, even if I'd bitten my nails down to the quick, exposing the meaty pad behind the hard, now torn shell to the point they'd throb, I would still find a way of making it worse. Instead of acknowledging the fact that if I left them alone entirely they'd heal and would likely stop hurting, something deep inside me thought I was doing important correctional work by removing the debris left behind by hurricanes of my own making. Again, my hands thought they were helping to tidy up the aftermath of the destruction they themselves had wrought, blissfully unaware they were in so doing perpetuating the cycle rather than tying it up for good. This 'just one more bite will make it right' mentality is what has made the once lightly-trodden road of my picking compulsion a well-worn track, an indelible scratch on my life. I'm surprised it hasn't turned up as a ridge on my palms' life-line, so strongly have my fingers written their own deranged story. A story that has become my story.

Nails

It makes me think of the poor hairdresser in Wolviston – a posh village up a curving bank whose base is marked by the Kings Arms pub and which we'd as teenagers crest on the way to the service-station McDonald's – who made an absolute mockery of a haircut I once had. Though I was born bald and Liv was born with a wild tuft of twisting black hair, as I grew my hair kept pace and was soon brushing my lower back, perfectly tousled and silky smooth. It was truly my crowning glory and the envy of passers-by.

The problem was, though, that it took a lot (a *lot*) of tears and tantrums to get it to the presentable state people witnessed. I look at the photos, often in sepia as was Mam's occasional tendency at the time, of me lying on my belly with my chubby cheeks cupped in balled hands as hair tumbled like water all around me, and I think *yeah, right*. I remember the knots that mane would invisibly harbour, only shockingly revealed when Mam came in with a brush and started going at them. She didn't mean for it to pull, would press her hand against smoothed roots to make it tug as little as possible, but so much hair with so many knots meant that, no matter how hard she tried, the experience would against her best, fading hopes go the same way every time: with me shrieking at the top of my lungs, sitting there defeated and acting as though she was the cruellest, most evil parent seen outside a Disney film. I played the martyr, but I was always a nightmare about my hair.

Before school, Grandma Mary would sometimes come round and brush my hair, probably giving an exhausted

Mam a well-deserved break. I'd request so much of her, like she was my own personal stylist, such as one plait on the left side of my head and one pigtail, left unplaited, on the right. God knows what my teachers thought. At other times I'd experiment with bunches that had bobbles all the way down so they were a sort of semi-braid. If there was a single bump on my crown, travelling the necessarily smooth route to wherever the bobble was to be tied that day, I'd (bless her heart) make her start again. Mam, whose hair was once the spitting image of Sharon Osbourne's (spiky and red-streaked), was surely to blame. She took an immense, almost neurotic, pride in her hair, backcombing it before teasing it with the pointy metal end of the comb in different directions, ploughing it with TRESemmé ultra-hold hairspray after she'd tonged it into uniform submission in the downstairs mirror by the stairs. Hair was clearly something that mattered a great deal, and far be it from me to embarrass the family by having unruly kinks in my hairdo. No, the ponytail had to be scraped so tightly back that my forehead went with it and probably made me look like I'd had botched plastic surgery. Sometimes my scalp would scream with it all day. Then I knew I looked perfect.

Eventually, it all got too much for my team of stylists and Mam opted to take me to the hairdressers to get me a shorter 'do. I was about nine or ten at the time, I think, so it had been a long road to get here, and, looking back, I'm madly impressed by how long they put up with me and my mane. She drove me up the hill to the hairdresser's at the top, a hairdresser that, flanked by cute village houses, had a satisfyingly provincial and bespoke aura about it. I was optimistic. Inside were piles of the shiny hair magazines Mam often had at home. Liv and I always marvelled and balked at the unbelievable, sometimes gravity-defying, styles. Surely these couldn't be real women who'd chosen to do that to their hair? They'd have fringes but with one uncut section as long as the rest of the head of hair, covering one eye like a curtain. How could that be comfortable? Sitting there cross-legged, leafing through one of these and tutting, must've seen me fit right into that salon. 'Ee, surely a woman with so beautiful a face wouldn't ruin it by cutting her hair into a platinum blonde bowl cut that goes down to her nose? I'd be mortified!'

I was sure they had to be wigs, so while I was excited to see these manic manuals splayed out among *Hello* and *Heat* on the glass table by the waiting sofa, I was also very aware my hair was not a wig and that such an attack on my 'do couldn't be so easily walked back. I was nervous, but Mam reassured me as I drank my complimentary orange juice that it was going to be a lovely haircut, nothing too drastic, and that it would be so much more manageable. And I was growing up. I felt the experience was a milestone somehow, an entrance into womanhood that meant I'd be leaving the salon not only with a different hairstyle but as a different, less knotty and tangled, person.

I was in the chair for a long time and would glance back at an eager Mam, catching her eye in the mirror as she'd gesture in reassurance. 'It looks good' she'd smile with her eyes, occasionally raising a thumbs-up if she thought I was looking especially unsure. I watched the handfuls of hair fall and splay on the floor around me and with every passing minute felt a creeping sense of doom. Mam suddenly wasn't looking so smiley, but rather eagle-eyed and on edge. Her reflected face had got closer, hadn't it, since I'd first glimpsed it an hour or so ago? And then, what was this? Mam was getting up? Fuck. She was never afraid to complain, be that in the Hartlepool TK Maxx; a restaurant like the Italian we went to in Middlesbrough – Fellinis; or the hairdresser's. Ever a sucker for a bargain and well aware of her consumer rights, she'd definitely say if the steak was undercooked, or the top had been ten quid cheaper last time she was in or, as I was about to find out, that we'd agreed (she and the hairdresser had agreed) that it wouldn't be this short.

Mam had woken up out of standby mode and asked them what they were doing, that this isn't what we'd asked for. It transpired that the stylist was either somewhat new or incompetent, it didn't matter, and they quailed in the face of my formidable mother. Herself pretty capable with a pair of hairdressing scissors, brimming with knowledge gleaned from magazines and a life spent with two sisters and two girls, she instructed the woman very carefully what to do next.

I mention this moment because it reminds me of my hands' desire to even up the self-inflicted damage already caused, consciously or not. The skittish stylist just, I suppose, kept cutting, standing back to see if it was even, finding it wasn't, and snipping away some more until the bob got higher and higher and higher. The same ritualistic evening-up would disastrously play out with a pair of tweezers and my eyebrows not too long after.

Eventually my mam called a stop to the charade and, I'm pretty sure, we left without paying. The cycle of my nail biting, and later my skin picking, followed a similar trajectory, except I've yet to leave without paying. No, for now I'm still both sitting in the seat and, appraising my work, wielding the scissors, trying to make right what went so very wrong somewhere along the way.

When I was still in Key Stage One my nails got so bad that a new approach was taken. I clearly wasn't going to stop on my own. If anything, my behaviour was escalating to the point where it hurt to hold a pencil. So a special and purposefully revolting nail polish was purchased by Mam especially for me. I remember Mam holding my hand out and painting the clear gloopy liquid over my little nails (even littler given how low they'd been bitten, only their white crescent moons still partially visible), taking care to purposefully cover very slightly the area around the nail, which was, she knew, one of the worst areas. Once a nail was gone, or else no more could be ripped from it, I'd start biting the skin around the edges until they bled. When they did bleed I only bit more, like a shark scenting blood.

I don't think my mam was shocked when she discovered I actually quite enjoyed the bitter taste of the polish.

I imagine it was more of an eye-roll 'of course you do' reaction that squared perfectly with my weird and unpredictable childhood quirks. I don't remember what it tasted like – I imagine a sort of Marmitey flavour – but honestly it wouldn't have mattered. I think I would have continued regardless, if only out of a stubbornness that I could do whatever I wanted – no methods could work on me because I could see through The Matrix.

Even with my skin picking, I act paranoid as though the world is out to get me. I snarl dismissively and snobbishly at the self-care my therapist suggests, explaining that the rampant commercialisation of mental health is actually a scourge on society, and while I appreciate mud masks might work for some people, I unfortunately can't get on board with such a neoliberal approach to mental illness and disorders. She can barely get a word in between my breaths to say it doesn't have to be that and maybe I should just, you know, go for a walk every other day or something. It's a defence mechanism, I think, this urge to outsmart and out-act the 'superiors' trying to help me and to cower behind a ruthless independence that's really a fear of being split open even wider.

I'm special, I'd think, and so your remedies and therapies won't be able to deal with such a complex person with such complex problems. Greatness is always misunderstood, after all. I wasn't aware then, but I'm very aware now of the dark lustre of the 'mental turmoil fuels art' myth. This intended isolationism, the forged belief that I could hide behind a hollow, self-inflated sense of self and a gold-starred intelligence masked a fear of being seen. If I was apart from others, I couldn't be understood or helped by them. Too bad. I can stay in my shadows doing the things that destroy and sustain me, whether nibbling non-existent nails or ravaging a face, because you can't stop me.

It was a fear that what was being suggested wouldn't work and then I really would be fucked. A reluctance to actually try, in case, well, in case I was incurable. A paradoxical reluctance, since to be incurable would be to be apart, different. In this reluctance was a desire to be seen that couldn't admit to itself. I was scared I'd end up lost in the maze rather than overlooking it from a safe distance. Basically, I was born a stroppy teenager who insists they're misunderstood, and have remained this terrifyingly pubescent newborn ever since. *Leave me alone, mom, but also look after me because I'm a little baby who can't look after herself.*

These types of behaviours, skin picking and the like, are often referred to as being self-soothing, so I'm probably not too far off some fragment of truth about myself when I talk about defence mechanisms and protective tendencies. I've said before that skin picking makes me feel completely numb – I enter the zone and, as I describe it to my boyfriend and therapist, if I'm not too careful I 'get stuck' there. It's a way of neutralising negative emotions like anxiety and agitation, and the relief the release brings is addictive, is what turns it into a body-focussed *repetitive* behaviour. It's a trick mirror though. As soon as the sedative effect wears off, the only way to combat the threat is the very thing that constitutes the threat: as I come to consciousness, I realise in horror what I've done. The skin picking has made me boundlessly anxious and ashamed, and retreating back into its foggy embrace immediately eases my pain, my captor the first to save me.

My nail biting as it was then is what Dr Jerry Bubrick, a senior clinical psychologist at the Child Mind Institute, would probably call a functional body-focussed repetitive behaviour (BFRB), bordering on the compulsive dysfunctional. Nail biting can turn into a compulsive and dysfunctional iteration of a BFRB, but for me it erred on the lighter side of things – more an act of perfectionism and a desire to set right the damage previously caused. I didn't sit and do it for hours, focussed entirely on the all-consuming activity to the point I thought there was anything wrong with what I was doing (though I was, after all, a child), but I say it bordered on the compulsive because of how anxious a child I was and how desperately in need of soothing I was. In contrast to 'functional', I now fully occupy the 'compulsive' district (have a semi-detached there and a growing family), the derivation of which, Bubrick explains, 'is done to self-soothe or deal with anxiety or other negative emotions'. If I didn't quite know how close to the dark side I was then, I most certainly do now. I can't see shit. But we'll get to that.

What I saw when I glimpsed my hands that day in music assembly was red dots. Like Lady Macbeth, I looked down in abject horror at the multitudinous sea incarnadine therein. But instead of the blood of a king lately murdered, I saw raised red bumps lining my upturned palm, one at the base of each finger. I had never seen these raised mounds of deeper-coloured flesh before, and alarm bells immediately rang. Something was terribly wrong. My urgent need to attract emergency medical attention was momentarily countered by the opposing urge not to draw attention to myself, and I looked despairingly over at one of the teachers – the one whose ample breasts, constantly fighting to break free from low-cut T-shirts, would distract me during assembly (not sexually, just genuine jaw-dropping curiosity). She wasn't looking, and I tried my best to mutely catch her eye. I can't remember whether this unlikely tactic actually worked or whether I raised my hand, devastated, and was escorted out with the eyes of everyone burning into the back of my head.

What I do remember is sitting on the edge of one of the tables of the classroom out the double doors and down some stairs with a teacher seated sympathetically across from me. My three main thoughts were: 1. *I can't believe she's letting me sit on the table!* 2. *I sat perfectly upright during assembly for nothing, since I've now scuppered my chance at picking out any musical instrument from the trolley*, and 3. *There's something deeply wrong with my hands, I'm likely going to die and will never again hold a tambourine.* Out, out, brief candle.

A kind face with a bob straighter all the way round than the chop I was later subjected to in Wolviston village, the teacher patiently waited for me to stop crying and blubbering before asking me, gently, what was wrong. I held out my hand to show her the damned spots and braced myself for her to jump up in blood-curdling horror from the child-sized chair on which she perched. I was taken aback when she did no such thing. It may have even stemmed my steady stream of tears. Suppressing, I'm sure, a laugh, she smiled and showed me her own hand.

'Look,' she traced a finger with a perfectly shaped nail in a curve across her palm, 'I've got them too. Everyone has them; they're nothing to worry about. Sometimes they get a little redder than usual if we are hot or if, for example, you've been grabbing something like monkey bars.'

Surprisingly, I don't remember feeling the acute humiliation I'd expect my small self to have felt. I think it was just genuine relief. Now all there was to be upset about was the raucous cacophony of musical instruments ringing from the hall. It only lasted for around eight minutes, though, and then with the rumbling of eager footsteps we stampeded outside for playtime.

6
Spoon

The hills in Lisbon were killer. Tanned locals slouched in their shaded doorways drinking cold beer as the sun reached its blinding height, amusement twinkling in their eyes as they watched us foolish tourists walk the vertiginous city under beating, cloudless heat. They had watched many thousands do the same and would surely watch thousands more. Only after a couple of exhausting days of well-intentioned exploration did we realise, or decide to accept, that between noon and three there really was nothing for it but to nap and lounge around our Airbnb or duck into a bar for something tall with ice in.

We were following Google Maps up winding cobbled roads lined with deep tram tracks, turning round corners into dusty side streets that led us down where we'd just walked up, weaving sweatily and breathlessly through labyrinthine streets strung with colourful bunting and drying laundry. The scalp of my hair's parting roasted red and tingling. We were hunting for a contemporary art gallery buried somewhere in the city. Bright yellow trams slipped by us, full to the brim. We stopped for ice creams at a tiny shop before trudging onward, this way and that, wondering if we'd ever stumble upon our destination.

When we did, it didn't look like much, just a white sign outside a building blending in with the rest. I couldn't really complain, anyway. The idea of planning anything fills me with pure dread (the idea of doing anything that requires any effort fills me with pure dread), and while I try not to take the piss out of my co-holidayers by dutifully picking out one or two things to add to the agenda, I generally ride holidays from the backseat. I'm lucky, really, to be surrounded by people with an appetite for scheduling days around landmarks and bars they've read about, cafes, art galleries. My university friends were (are) to me shining beacons of sophistication and good taste, and were (are) better at this stuff than me anyway. I'm happy if the flights are cheap and the food good. But crucially, cheap.

And hey, listen, I have good taste too, OK? I know that Jeff Koons' 'art' is 'garbage' (I didn't hire 'studio serfs' to write this for me, promise) and that (think, Lauren, think) Georgia O'Keefe's isn't. But on my most anxious days, the many potentialities of the day clamour loudly to the front of my mind from the second I wake up, as though I've slept through the most catastrophic event in history, and also I'm President of Earth.

Imagine that scene in *Bruce Almighty* where Jim Carrey has to dash out of the fancy restaurant's side door because the sound of everyone's prayers overwhelms him. The choice paralysis of what to have for breakfast (*I really want this, ah but it's not very healthy, but you've had a hard week, you'll regret having used the milk when it runs out, yes but that's what milk is for? Whatever, it will always run out and anyway while I've got you, what are you going to do after that, Lauren? Ey? What the fuck are you gunna do then? Have lunch?*) is sometimes bad enough. For me, a true holiday is a holiday away from having to make decisions. To float on my back in the sea with my eyes closed and be carried freely, bobbing on the tide. Holidays as a kid were always prefaced with the word 'package', a combination which, as I got older, I internally scoffed at as tacky, inauthentic, touristy. As an adult burdened by life's relentless bureaucracy, its TV licences and pension funds and council tax, I understand why people go on all-expenses-paid cruises where their days are mapped out for them, their breakfast decided, their brains taken care of by those whose job it is.

So sure, I'll do a rudimentary search for things that, fair enough, I'd genuinely be happy to do and see. But if we follow through with said plans and my friends don't like the medieval castle I pick (they won't exhibit any signs that the time's being wasted by my stupid choice, but I'll find traces of it in their faces), I'll take it as personally as if I were the master builder.

I remember the door being low enough that even I had to duck, and inside the walls were white. A woman who looked at us like she hadn't seen other people in a millennium enthusiastically welcomed us inside and gestured with the sweep of a braceleted arm towards another room, as if to say 'Come in, come in. Please. It's been seven years since last I gazed 'pon human eyes.' That being the entirety of the gallery – those two low rooms, empty but for us and the friendly Portuguese lady – we had to really take our time soaking up every piece, not only to make our long journey here worthwhile but also to make sure we didn't leave too soon as to be rude. The art, as I remember it, was what you might call conceptual. Cerebral. Either that or the panting heat had seeped into my senses and I was hallucinating what I thought I saw before me. But no matter how hard I tried to compose myself, to read into the art vulnerability, fragility, the precariousness of life, in a way, all I saw was a spoon suspended on its belly over a metal wire. Like Rose from *Titanic* leaning over the railings to look at the propellers, but a plain metal spoon.

The thickish wire was held up by metal stands on either side – a tightrope – and the spoon balanced perfectly still in the middle of it. I stood, hands held behind me, looking at the thing with a faux-furrowed brow as the diorama screamed 'I am a spoon balanced on a wire' at me. Was the artist mocking me? Was the piece a criticism of the egotistical need to 'get something' out of a piece of art that we can then attribute to the brilliant acuity of our intellectual third eye, our unique ability to see through to the heart of the thing and catch, lo! a glimpse of *art*? In thinking this, had I won? Or had it ensnared me with a triumphant 'Gotcha! I am a spoon balanced on a wire, fool!'? An encounter had happened, was taking place that very moment, and I wasn't and am not altogether sure it was a friendly one. Here I was, come to glance upon some art, ready to have my feathers fluffed, and this spoon balanced on a wire had the audacity – the *audacity* – to question my motives? *I'm here for you, spoon balanced on a wire; I climbed mountains, thighs screaming, to find you, and for what? You find me lacking? Well, son, I find you lacking.*

What is it about art that is begging to be touched, anyway? What's with that? This spoon was *dying*, positively gagging, to be wobbled off its perch. I was dying to oblige. I remember in 2015 when a 12-year-old Taiwanese boy tripped on a wire ostensibly to keep visitors a safe distance away and accidentally punched a whopping hole through a $1.5m painting. Turns out putting said wire at ankle height wasn't the cleverest design choice. Once I'd seen the story, I couldn't get enough. I went through every single news article about it – BuzzFeed, Business Insider, Bored Panda (I don't know either) – scouring the web for every scrap of delicious coverage I could snaffle. It wasn't, I promise, because I'm a deviant who enjoys child-specific *Schadenfreude* (although what is *You've Been Framed!* if not this?), but because I'd dreaded that very specific moment one way or another my entire life. The glass tipped, ketchup squeezed, coach stopped, thing *done*, actually done! A universal intake of breath, the fabric finally ripped to reveal … what? I was sure I detected something other than an innocent trip-up in the footage, something in the way the child fell looked to me ... intentional, I was sure of it, and I soaked up every second of understanding. Sometimes the what ifs are just too loud. I wanted to hold the boy to me, to stroke his hair in a reassuring embrace, but also to whisper in his ear – 'I see you're one of us. I know what you did. But don't worry, I'll never tell' – before disappearing into the crowd with the swoop of a trench coat.

The first time I visited London was on a coach trip aged 13 or 14, after Liv and I were singled out as poor but deserving by our school's art department and invited along for free. We were giddy little maniacs the whole trip, egged on by our friend Amy Black, whose angel-faced mischief and wicked sense of humour drove us completely wild. I can't remember a moment when we weren't laughing; from the second one of the beds collapsed in our grim little hotel room, our bellies racked with the pain of it. It would take only a sidelong glance at each other while the teacher was talking to set us off again like fireworks.

The big city didn't seem real, felt like a whirling technicolour film set erected just for us, and arm in arm we skipped through Piccadilly Circus, Russell Square, Leicester Square, all the squares, Madame Tussaud's (Amy was *very* excited to see the Justin Bieber waxwork), *Mamma Mia!* the musical, museums, the lot. On the way to a restaurant for tea one evening, I walked through a plume of my ex-boyfriend's cologne. My first love cloaked in Lynx! Surely it couldn't be? It wasn't, obviously, but I burst into tears, nonetheless. Yet earth-shattering heart-break gave way to quick-winged elation as easily as the shrugging off of the coats we draped onto the back of our dining chairs, finding delirious, so *random*, hilarity in the name of the dish 'pizza cotto'. That trip was one of the most wonderful I've ever had. For a brief, dazzling moment I forgot myself, caught up in life's current, feeling every second of it uninterrupted by myself.

That is, apart from one moment in the British Museum. We were rather excitingly being trailed by a security guard, having been correctly identified as nuisances due to our uncontrollable, loud giggles at anything resembling a penis. We were touching things signs explicitly told us not to touch and we were high on it: a group of usually-goody-two-shoes being scouted by the FBI. Spurred on by each other, the guard's subtle but unmistakable presence behind us made the museum a game. Away from home, trusted (wrongly) by the teacher to split off into groups, we were different, more daring versions of ourselves, drunk on independence.

That is, until one of us very nearly barrelled into a huge bust perched atop a modest marble plinth in the middle of one of the rooms. In the end, whichever one of us grazed it didn't make any perceivable impact – the thing didn't wobble, at least not to the naked eye, indeed barely registered the slight might of whoever's body had touched it. But I imploded with anxiety on impact. Our physics teacher had told us once that even when we thought we could feel our bums on our seats, we weren't actually touching the seat but microscopically levitating; that atoms created an unbreachable albeit minuscule gap between us and all things. This thing's atoms barely shivered, I'm sure of it, but I knew they were there and that somewhere an unstoppable vibration had sprung like a slinky into motion.

It rushed through me, like electricity. You'd think we were in the middle of robbing a bank the way my mood snapped. *We're in too deep, you guys*, I thought, stunned into sudden good behaviour and an eagerness to find the rest of our group. For the rest of the day my thoughts were as uncontrollable as storm-churned waves. As we sat eating what were to us obscenely expensive and disgusting sandwiches (our naive pallets were at that time unacquainted with avocado and were deeply unimpressed), I thought about the plinth, couldn't stop thinking about the plinth, about what could've unfolded and what sequence of devastating events would've been set into motion if the unimaginable had happened. *What if, what if, what if.* As we walked, more solemnly in my case, through the rest of the museum, every plinth fizzed with energy it seemed only I could see, as though I'd been cursed with the unenviable superpower of seeing the dizzying, destructive possibilities that silently lay therein: taunting me, teasing me, begging me to just tap it. There was that voice again, willing me to end it all. Just to get the inevitable out the way. The familiar building urgency surged in me, but this was no ketchup sachet.

Shit had got too real, especially (crucially) because, in the end, it hadn't. Just as I wouldn't have needed the toilet if there was a functional one on the coach, I wouldn't have had such a fierce, all-consuming urge to touch if touching wasn't forbidden. Like the unrolling of a Fruit Winder reveals, square by square, the comic wound therein, I was sure that with every frame that became visible (curse not being able to see the future) only terrible things would flood my vision. Only I could see the terrible dangers all around me, the terrible dangers that whispered to me from the inside of plinths, shelves of wine, pots of complimentary condiments. The Simon of my nightmarish game of Simon Says (*do this, do this, do this, do this, what if, what if, what if*) would be forgotten in ecstatic moments, lost for the most part in the many long hours of that trip.

But as the summer of my childhood faded, it was increasingly Simon I'd see when I looked in the mirror, his eyes looking out of mine. His voice began to sound a lot like my own, to take over my mind. Just when I'd think he'd moved on, an object or person or thing would fizz with that terrible, frantic energy. I'd feel it like a cliff edge I hadn't realised I'd been walking so close to, suddenly plummeting beneath me without warning, sending icy shockwaves through my blood. 'Look,' he'd say, 'that few days or weeks of calm? That was an illusion. But this is really you, this is reality. And something unthinkable is about to happen.'

* * *

I touched the spoon, obviously. With the stealth of a seasoned crook, I glimpsed over my shoulders at the backs of my friends, who were gazing intently at another piece, and thankfully not at me. The woman at the front desk had gone back to her computer and the coast was clear – I could see that – but surely they could hear how fast my heart was pounding, or even feel it beneath their thin-sandaled feet? My mouth was dry and I tried to push my anxiety, my Simon, back down, but it was over before it even started, just as soon as I saw 'Spoon Balanced on Wire'. Like I say, it was a Venus flytrap, begging to be touched by a fly unable to defy its immovable nature. With a gulp I touched it with the pad of my forefinger, heavier than I'd have liked, and it proper wobbled. The tragic satisfaction hit me quick (this shit was pure), and I hung suspended, time slowed to an almost-halt, in the moment I'd just ripped wide open. One nanosecond it looked like it would tip onto its heavy, round head, the next see-sawing so its tail stretched down.

'Let's go,' someone said, and my friends filed out of the small space before I could see how the thumb-flicked coin would land. *No no no no no no no no no no no*. Numb, I trailed behind them, the spoon still wobbling undecided, torturously vibrating out of my control, atoms dispersed in a thunderclap. But wait. Wasn't this my ideal scenario? I'd never have to see this woman again, and the spoon wasn't made of glass and surely could be propped back up? No potential buyers, if indeed this piece was destined for sale, would ever have to know the spoon's secret story, its chaotic, fizzing heart. I was off the hook, surely? I'd done what I had to do and, what joy, had got away with it!

The relief, I realised, was in the consequences: being covered in ketchup, told off by my mam for spilling another pint of juice all over the sticky pub table, stopping the coach, smashing a centuries-old bust, ruining an artwork.

The relief, I realised, was in the horrible thing actually happening. The cure – I felt right down to my marrow – lay in the very vague but looming event I felt on the horizon like death. By doing the thing before it could happen naturally, I was rider of the winds! Confounder of the fates! Like getting all my future wee out now, I wanted to feel all the worst feelings in that moment, to get them out of the way, like exams. If I tricked myself into really believing that a late text back meant someone had died, I'd surely be more prepared if it actually did happen. I was impatiently, frenetically building an armour out of heartbreak, tragedy, fear. I couldn't wait for it to develop naturally. After all, I didn't know how much time I had.

By refusing to fall and ruin my life, the spoon had ruined my life. That fucker. Now, my fate remained in the future and the coin had not fallen. The entire enterprise had been to get what felt like an inevitability out of the way (I couldn't have just *not* done it, because, what if?) and from that monster's limbs (so close to being vanquished!) sprang yet bigger, worse monsters threatening horrors each greater than the last. The words floated unbidden into my eyes: What if she comes running down the street after us now? What if it fell and broke and she found out where we were staying and billed it to me, bankrupting me for life? What if the police stopped me at the airport before I could get on my plane? Oh, good God, I'm never going to see my family again!

The worst of the heat had passed as we stepped out onto the street, or at least that's how it felt. Maybe it had just been stuffy in those windowless rooms, but my palms were still sweaty as we went on our way. That evening we went to a fancy restaurant, expertly chosen by one of my friends. It was located, I think, in an old but grand hospital building and had a medical theme that I thought wouldn't work but did. The plates were small and the food expensive, but sitting at the big round table on a mezzanine outside I felt the stirrings of calm. *But the spoon, the spoon, the spoon*, my mind railed. Again I felt like I was running from the disaster that had failed me into the path of a yet-unseen disaster. Wine-drunk and tired, I was relieved when we eventually went to bed.

That Taiwanese boy's story was a tonic and a curse. I could watch the whole thing play out, see how the penny dropped, from a safe distance. *So this is what happens*, I thought. *This is it*. Finally, disaster had struck and I could spy through my cliff-edge telescope the devastation of 'the thing happening'. Of course, I wished no ill will on the boy. Like I said, I felt a profound empathy for him, yet it was tinged by a jealousy I couldn't explain – that he'd done it, inadvertently or otherwise, that he was experiencing what I'd only dreamt of. And something like anger; that he didn't get in trouble, despite the objective reality of the situation, didn't feel right. He'd punched a hole in Paolo Porpora's oil on canvas *Flowers* and lived out what the *Guardian* called 'a slapstick nightmare' (is it too late to change the title of this book?). But it wasn't a slapstick nightmare, in the end, was it, because the organisers told the family they didn't have to pay for the restoration.

It was wrong, my mind felt. Something's not quite right. Not in any literal sense – I agree wholeheartedly that the boy deserved no repercussions, nor his family – but for it to be the event I'd waited for my entire life, the consequences had to be ruinous. Only then would I have experienced it properly, even vicariously. I was so prepared for the fatal blow that I felt disappointed and confused when it didn't come. This can't have been it, then – fantasy and delusion winning over reason. This can't be The Event because if it was The Event I've been dreading all this time then his life would have been ruined. Ignoring what was right there in front of me, I changed the story to fit my mind.

It was glaringly obvious, then, that there was an 'other side' to even life's worst calamities that didn't involve the worst. I'd experienced it myself, for God's sake – even when I was shouted at for spilling my drink, I got over it, I endured it and time elapsed, became history. Even if the spoon had fallen, the woman could've just said 'Please don't touch the displays' and that would've been the end of it. Hell, my mam had never mentioned anything about having to pay for that entire wall of wines I smashed. *But*, the voice volunteered, *next time, well, next time Mam's bollocking would be worse*. I'd make excuses, trip up on my own barrelling logic. *Maybe Mam's just in a good mood today. Maybe I didn't tip the glass properly, so it didn't count. Oh God, I'll have to do it again just to check. Smash something else*. I'd decided the Taiwanese boy's experience was a fluke. Simon was getting stronger, and for now the woods would continue to obstruct my view of the trees.

Something else lingered in the back of my mind, too. He was just a child. I'd been just a child when I was forgiven for acting out, acting weird. But adults, well, adults were supposed to have it together. When I wanted to be on *The X Factor*, part of the reason I cried so furiously was because every year I didn't apply I was another year older, and to my mind another year away from being a child superstar. It was very important to me that the judges should be surprised at how big my talent was for someone so young. I'd watched the show before, I'd seen *Britain's Got Talent*, I knew what the people wanted. Adults were impressive. Kids were *really* impressive. Through racking sobs I explained to Mam: 'But. The. Judges. Won't. Care. When. I'm. An. Adult. Because. Then. I'll. Be. Less. Impressive. To. Them.' I'd seen homeless people on the streets. If it was a child squatting in the entryway to a shop, begging for food, it seemed to me they'd be whipped up into someone's arms immediately.

Such things were unacceptable, but adults walked by adults in need like they were already ghosts.

In Portugal that not-so-fateful day, I was in my head still that anxious child – I still am – but I knew when I touched that spoon that I would unlikely be forgiven so soon. Every year that slipped by I felt more in danger as I grew out of the right to be scared. According to the *Guardian*'s coverage of that boy, a similar situation happened in 2012 in Dublin, where a man was sentenced to six years in jail for damaging a Monet painting estimated to be worth £7 m. It didn't say whether or not he'd tripped.

The coin flicked in the air that day in Lisbon still hasn't dropped. Not that I expect any repercussions to catch up with me now (that iconic meme of the girl trying kombucha? That was me as I wrote those words). What I mean is, I still don't know what the repercussions would be, not for *definite* (the definite lies only in experience, not reason or likelihood), so my experience of galleries … varies. Regardless of my mood, I can't resist getting up as close as possible to a painting so I can see the brush strokes, the dried globules of wet-looking paint, the flick of a signature in the corner. I eat it up with my eyes, touching with my mind, if not my hands, selfishly wishing I could run my fingers down each canvas while knowing that allowing people (even my ego knows I wouldn't be the chosen exception to the rule) to do so would mean the eventual destruction of the painting. Maybe all art is art begging to be touched, then. Maybe *art* lies in our inability ever to touch it, atoms preventing it like bums on seats as well as rules, without changing it somehow. Ruining it, at worse, transforming it, at best. Honestly, though, I don't really know the first thing about art. Other than the fact that I'd love to punch holes through it to see what's on the other side, and that that spoon was begging to be knocked off that wire.

7
Tooth

Before my skin there was my tooth. Or teeth, rather, if I really think about it. I've always had a distressing relationship with my teeth, one which stretches far beyond the usual dreams in which they crumble out one by one like feta cheese into my hand. I've already mentioned the way I used to compulsively bite down on my two front teeth in my anxious dance with Simon, which I'm sure had something to do with how they're now, near the bottom, almost see-through. When my dentist first told me about this when I was in my early to mid-teens, their translucence that is, I silently spiralled for weeks after. I was so angry and frustrated at myself, not least for not noticing the weakened enamel when it was right there in front of me. Why couldn't I look after myself? How could I fail at something so basic? I stopped drinking the two-litre bottle of fizzy pop I kept between Liv's bed and my bed for night-time slurps for a while, but eventually brought it back upstairs. After all, it was easier, wasn't it? Better than having to wash up a glass for water, so my empty, lazy, teenage reasoning went.

I too quickly forgot the feeling of disappointment, loss, irreversibility. After every check-up and every little filling,

I'd try to clutch those feelings like rotten pearls unexpect-edly unstrung, urging myself this time to change my habits before I did irreparable damage, before they clattered and bounced off, slipped between the floorboards. With every throb or sudden, unexpected flash of pain on biting down, I felt utterly, miserably, out of control. *Things have got out of hand*, my mind rasped. *There's no going back now*. When I eventually slipped back into the bad habits that had brought me here – stopping, for example, at the shop on the way home from school to buy pop and sweets and 20p bags of BBQ-flavoured crisps – the voice remained, but grew fainter, like the pain, the further away from the appointment I got. Nobody can think about their teeth *all* the time, after all.

And then, lo and behold, I'd find myself once again beneath a muted screen playing *Finding Nemo*, goggled and numbed and tilted back while drills whirred in my head. My anxiety burst into flame when it came to my teeth, and after every appointment I'd have a not-so-secret cry. Why couldn't I get my dentist's words to stick to me? Instead, they temporarily clung like dandelion spurs, eventually, inevitably, dispersed. They'd drop off without me even realising it. In the immediate aftermath of each appointment, I'd spend minute after minute in front of the mirror on Mam's landing, prying open my lips and checking them: first a grimace, checking the transparency of my two front teeth against the row below, then parting them slightly to see them alone (the harsh landing light surely making the vision all the more ghastly), then unhinging my jaw to try and see all the way to the back. Sometimes fillings slipped out and I'd swallow them without noticing, or, worse, I'd crunch down on them in horror. I dreaded the moments I'd end up back in that cursed chair with a grown man's plastic-gloved fingers pushing down on my spongy teeth to gauge their pain level. I winced as he brought that synthetic blue-gloved smell closer to my face. Maybe it was because I'd been uncontrollably driving myself, at home, to press down hard on the bits that hurt, as if to pre-empt the pain the next time it came unbidden. I knew it would hurt, but some deep lunge in me made me do it. *Get it out of the way now.* That was the reasoning. Again, I was trying and failing to trick time. Instead of helping, which they thought they definitely were, my hands were causing more and more damage. Still, I pressed down, harder and harder. Testing myself.

When it finally came to the dentist's hand prodding around in there, it was fully and immediately clear that my surreptitious pre-emptive pokes hadn't had the effect I'd hoped: to prevent future pain by feeling that pain now, in a way I could control (pressing down was as hard as I wanted it to be). Wanted isn't the right word, perhaps needed. I was an Olympian in training, trying to push myself beyond my limits, except I wasn't getting better at anything the more I did it. No, I was somehow getting worse.

Eventually, the words I'd been trying to stave off were uttered: 'We're going to have to take it out.' OK, it wasn't that blunt. On the upper left side of my gums, my second from last tooth was dying. I was about 14 or 15 and a root canal hadn't stopped the pain, which doesn't make sense now I say it out loud but there we are, that is how I remember it working. The ginger-haired dentist (who at the time I thought was hot, but then again I was at the age where I thought everyone was hot, especially pretty much all grown men) explained that he could go back in there and have another jiggle about or, and he was so sorry, take it out.

I went into reassuring mode, if you could call it that, as if he was the one in the big white seat and not me. 'Don't say sorry!' I said. 'Don't worry at all, I totally understand [who the fuck was talking with my mouth?], let's just take it out. It's easier that way, isn't it?' The sudden nonchalance! Was I trying to impress him, this average-looking ginger man (but ugh, a man! hot) with my lack of fucks? Nothing, I've learnt since, is sexier than a woman who doesn't care if her permanent last-chance teeth get pliered from her skull forever. It's a marvel he managed to get through the procedure at all without orgasming.

Things started going south as soon as he started. Firstly, being injected with a needle in the gums is the stuff of the *Saw* franchise. Nobody should have to go through that – it's obscene and should be illegal. The gums are an abomination of human design. They're just so *gummy*. Like, is it skin? Bone covered in muscle? Bone covered in skin? There's just something irretrievably grim and unthinkable about them, which is fine given that in daily life I've been lucky enough not to have to think about them very much at all – they do their job more or less well in terms of keeping my teeth in my head, but Christ alive, they have the makings of a really brilliant and surprisingly as yet unseen *Doctor Who* monster. A person who's gum all over? I'd rather die. Even the dentist prodding them with a begloved forefinger was bad enough, so I scrunched my eyes closed as he raised the needle and brought it into my cavernous mouth. I felt the cold needle like a sharp pinch and shivered as it slipped deeper inside; from then on I was stiff as a board. That should've been the worst of it, he'd said as much before he started – 'Just a sharp pinch and then numb, you'll hardly feel a thing' – but of course it wasn't. I did feel a thing, a really horrific not-in-the-agreement thing. As soon as he started to thumb-plunge the syringe's contents into me, I felt an electric spark rip like lightning across my entire face. I was stunned.

'All good?' he asked.

'No', I explained. 'That just electrocuted my entire fucking face actually.'

'Ah, OK.' He'd hit a nerve, he explained, and then hit another one by audaciously claiming that this was *a good thing* because now the numbing agent would work faster. I didn't believe that for one second, but after that one second I very much did, as the left side of my face departed the land of the living and sagged like meat. I'd enjoy prodding it later, but for now, the extraction (that's what he called it, like it was some precious jewel being plucked from the earth and not the corrupt popcorn it was).

Reader, it got worse. Within minutes the drill head had spun off its whizzy electrical buzzy thing and into my mouth, clattering against teeth I, on the left-hand side, couldn't feel, and on the right-hand side, could. The dentist, even after Nerve-gate, remained remarkably calm and nonchalant at this occurrence, in my memory just refitting the nozzle onto the uncontrollable snake it muzzled, before going back in. Anyone who's been to the dentist for Intensive Work will know how weird it feels to have someone drilling your teeth when they're numb. You can feel them pulling, tugging the difficult bits, but there's no pain. Just the sense that someone is rearranging your skull, and the drug that was supposed to put you to sleep under the goggled glare of the Frankensteinian maniac who's kidnapped you hasn't worked.

I should add that it was around this time in my life, when the glossy real-life mags covered Mam's rug, that I read a story in one of said magazines about a Woman Who Had Surgery and FELT IT ALL. Once I started reading it, I was incapable of tearing my eyes away, like it was some horrific car crash I couldn't help but want to see in all its gory detail, and it just got worse and worse. I could feel the words entering my memory like shards, every subsequent one slashing open another neural pathway. Whichever drug was meant to paralyse her worked, so she was incapable of so much as opening her eyes, but whatever was supposed to put her to sleep hadn't, so she was alive and kicking up there while they opened her belly and started rummaging around inside. She felt everything, she said, and was (obviously!) completely traumatised by the experience. And listen, I don't understand anaesthetics or whether they're supposed to paralyse you or what, but I do know that that shit is not supposed to happen – period. I was always worried that this would happen to me in the dentist's chair, that the drill would touch nerve before I'd screamed loud enough to stop him. That I'd feel the nerve exposed, screaming, to the cool, air-conditioned air.

Thankfully, I remained numb throughout. When it was finally over he stuffed a marshmallowy substance into the hole and got me to bite down on it before sending me on my merry way.

My grandma always came to the dentist with me, knowing how I was with it, and afterwards we went and sat down somewhere. I tried having a cup of tea, waiting for it to cool, but still wound up burning myself anyway. We enjoyed the ridiculousness of my numb face – Liv, who was also there, took a video of me talking out of a laughing, wonky smile, which did well on Facebook – but after a time the jocularity wore off and I realised what to me was the gravity of what I'd just done.

The dentist had explained to me that because of the way light works, and how the back of my mouth was dark, no one would be able to tell even if I laughed with my head flung backwards. Even if I was on the waltzers and my neck gave up and my head dragged back. But now the numbness was wearing off, I could *feel* the newly empty space, not just in a physical with-my-poking-tongue kind of way, but with over-eager tendrils of compulsive thought. I prodded and brushed the absence and felt I'd lost something huge. Tears – you guessed it – streamed and streamed where once there had been only laughter. I turned to my grandma and heaved 'When my skeleton is found by *Time Team* or whatever, they'll see there was a tooth missing and think badly of me,' before breaking down in sobs again.

My mind was filled with my skeleton, my previously lovely skeleton – how could I not have realised how lovely it was before? How *stupid* of me not to, how *stupid*. *Stupid*. Apparently I didn't care enough about it to keep it in pristine condition for future archaeologists, who I was sure would care enormously. Now they would assume me a peasant with a poor diet (*Can they find cherry coke in the chemical composition of teeth? Oh God, even if they can't now, they will be able to by then,* etcetera). In many ways they'd be right, of course, about the cherry coke (Asda's own), but at least before then they might have at least *considered* the possibility I was of royal lineage and worthy of a museum vitrine.

The enormity of what I'd done, egregious as murder, plagued me as we made our way home. I went straight upstairs to inspect the absence in the long mirror on the landing, where the lightbulb was bright and orange and unforgiving. Back in the days when Liv and I would go to house parties, the Apple Sourz days, we'd get Mam to take 100 pictures each and then a few together on her digital camera before we went: hands on bony hips, fringes pulled to the side, lipstick-smothered half-smiles eclipsed by extraordinarily short skirts. The landing was, for me, lowest on the pecking order of potential photo-shoot spots. Best of all was the slightly gloomy hallway downstairs, in front of the porch window – enough to get *some* natural light, but not nearly enough to illuminate what I actually looked like, which would be unaccept-able. Sometimes there'd be no good photos in the heaving stack. Mam would bear the brunt of her frustration – it was obviously her fault that we looked exactly like ourselves in the photographs.

Here, though, hooking my cheek with a finger like a doomed fish, I didn't think I'd ever get a picture taken again. I might not ever leave the house. I'd chucked the blood-soaked marshmallowy thing into the toilet by this point, and the puckered and bloody little absence I saw made me want to vomit. I spat pink spit into the sink, and then I went back to the mirror to keep looking. I don't know what else I expected to see; I wanted to feel the full gravity of it, for it to somehow 'hit me' (as though it hadn't already). Exhausted with all the inspecting, I saun-tered like an empty tracksuit downstairs and into the dining room. I slumped down at the dining table and spun the black, looping cord of the phone around my fingers. Mam finally surrendered her silence and acknowledged me – I'd no doubt been performatively huffing and sigh-ing in her general direction – and told me it really wasn't that big of a deal because no one would see it, and as the dentist had reassured me, as I grew older the gap would likely become smaller as my other teeth crowded in.

'Can you see it if I laugh?' I asked, tilting my head back and laughing with a caricature face. She tutted, her tone getting higher, incredulous, at the end. 'When have you ever, has anyone, ever laughed like that? You can't see it anyway you daft get, oway.' But I didn't follow her into the living room, just stayed there silent-crying – the kind of crying where you've got your head in your arms and your mouth open in a voiceless howl dripping saliva – thinking about how the only thing going for me, my fanciability, which I was still very much invested in, was suddenly gone. My head spun thick with the permanence of it, and I vowed never to drink pop or eat sweets or hard things or chocolate ever again, that this was rock bottom and the wake-up call I needed. But I did, as hastily as a diet begun on a Monday is dropped by Wednesday. Even before the painful gummy crevice was sealed shut I'd got over it, joining in with gusto a crisp-eating sesh at my friend Ellie's house. A shard of tangy cheese Dorito lodged itself in the gum, to my horror, and I had to extract it in her downstairs toilet, which I thereafter vomited into. Even that, though, slipped into the past, and whether the damage was already done or I'd created fresh damage, I found myself back at the dentist's a year or two later for another big procedure.

It was another of the chunky teeth, this time the second from the back on the lower right side, that was giving me grief. I'd tried to ignore it for as long as possible, not wanting to admit I'd gone back on my healthy pledge, but even biting down on soft food became an impossibility and I relented. Another root canal was needed. After the failed attempt at the first one, which had resulted in the extraction (in lieu of another crack at it), I was sceptical as hell. I asked lots and lots and lots of questions and probably delayed several other patients' appointments, but I needed absolute reassurance that this was going to work. He obviously couldn't give me that, he said, but he was confident that this wasn't the same as last time and the only way would be to try. That one, the upper left bastard, was cracked and would likely buckle under another root canal treatment. This one didn't look so bad.

By the time he'd finished, he hadn't taken out the full root. He'd done some other dental wizardry I won't try and remember nor explain that meant he'd gone down a few layers of strata, scooped out the minging stuff, and left a very thin layer of enamel over the frenetic nerve. It was a risk, he said, but one he was willing to take. Like a dilapidated house, he'd realised the foundations were actually still there, the bare bones as it were, and he was willing to do it up, restore it as close as possible to its former glory. He put over the top a temporary – though, he reassured me, sturdy – crown and, having taken a mould of the remaining, flattened half-tooth before doing so, invited me back to get my bespoke permanent crown fitted some time in the future.

A paradoxical character, for whom every tiny life occurrence simultaneously scars forever yet fails to create a lasting impression sufficient to change my behaviour, I took him at his word and bought a £1 packet of chorizo slices from the nearest supermarket. I headed to a nearby friend's house with them in hand, also clutching closely the justification that I needed to eat dinner, didn't I, and that I'd be fine if I just ate on one side. About three slices in, I failed. It turns out that it's really difficult to only use one side of the mouth to eat – it requires a significant amount of deft tongue work and razor-sharp concentration on the physical mechanics of eating only, at the expense of the deliciously smoky taste of Spanish sausage. I must have subconsciously been unwilling to make this sacrifice – and, in any case, unable, since it's hard to control a side of your face you can't feel – and the teeny tooth-topper pinged off. At first, I thought it was one of those weird white gristly bits you sometimes get in chorizo – the ones that unfortunately remind you exactly what it is you're eating – but then a throb burst through the numbness like a lamppost on a foggy night. The glue obviously hadn't set yet, and my tooth screamed. Tail between my legs, I slunk back to the dentist's and had another one put in. This time I ate whatever the adult equivalent of baby food is (soup, I guess) until I finally had a permanent bad boy fitted. For the first couple of weeks I re-entered a Googling-how-much-extensive-dental-work-such-as-veneers-and-bridges-costs phase.

Tooth

When the first tooth had been plucked out, not too long before, I'd been horrified in my research to discover that they had to file the healthy teeth around a gap into little shark's teeth in order to fit fake ones. I don't know why this surprised me. Like, how else would it work? But I sank further into despair; not only could I not afford such options, but they didn't bring my tooth back. But I did it again, pre-empting the inevitable moment this one would fall out and my crumbly feta dreams would edge closer to reality – a nerve grazing a thin layer of tooth that was surely unable to contain it.

I didn't shell out any money, and my remaining teeth were not filed into fangs. Three or four years passed.

The wind that close to the sky was ferocious, a feral beast always *just* out of sight, slashing around our heads and whipping our hair into watering eyes. Stone stairs, half-crumbled paneless windows, weather-worn walls, and crenellations like teeth comprised the breathless castle's husk, from whose impossibly high promontory others like it could be seen; ancient ships drifting between breaks in mist. It wasn't a particularly cold day. On the contrary, we'd wound through vineyard upon vineyard bathed in golden light to get here, Tom's expert driving manoeuvring us, then, up and around knife-edge turns – passing, ominously, the shell of a car pitched down a ditch – up and up, round and round we went, every sweep around a corner stealing our breath and widening our eyes. When we got to the top we – that is, me, my boyfriend Jovan, Tom (our friend) and Kate (also our friend and Tom's then-girlfriend, now wife) – had a picnic of questionable service-station sandwiches, sat at a lone picnic table above the world. Below us, it was huge and verdant and endless.

Finished, we turned again, faces skyward, to the cloud-surfing castle whose every corridor, staircase and stone we desperately wanted to inhabit, with whose history we wanted to interlace, mind and body. The climb was intense – I'd feel it in my legs tomorrow – but worth it. Oh, so very worth it. A vast, rolling carpet of every green, beige and brown tumbled before us as we peered through – or rather over the edge of – half windows, low walls. We gripped hard onto scant rope handrails and pressed our palms against the cold walls out of necessity as well as, at least for me, to feed that need – curling through me like warm tendrils reaching my fingertips, the thread of human history linking us all – to connect with whoever was here before. Whoever else touched this place, and this place, and this place. The open-air ruin – though, really, there was nothing ruined about it – was surprisingly short of visitors and I felt utterly alone up there, in the best way. Tom even found a secret – or what seemed to be a secret, which was good enough for me – passageway, which we trudged down with arched backs and lowered heads. I was so scared and so excited that I'm sure the adrenaline kept me warm for some time, kept me exploring. But then as though from nowhere the wind picked up in a great heaving bellow, and just how high up we were became terrible. We were so brutally exposed, so chilled to the bone by the air up here; Kate – slight, petite – carefully lowered herself onto a step sheltered by surrounding intact walls, and couldn't take a step further for panicked fear of being defenestrated. I continued on for a short time after, but quickly conceded. Once sat, it seemed impossible ever to get up again without being sucked through a passageway with the force of a plane door opening mid-flight, and, shocked through, we carefully – so carefully – exited the building back onto the sloping hill by which we had approached it.

Almost as soon as we stepped out of this Cathar castle, one of several we visited in the Languedoc region of France on that most magnificent of trips, the wind dropped. The series of walls, corridors and gloomy stairwells lit by slits of freezing light had acted like a conduit, channelling and powering the air in surges through itself. I thought with a chill of how many people over however many hundreds of years would've dropped to their deaths here, or whether the walls were strong enough to hold off the anger raging outside. There were hardly any ceilings now (I imagined them ripped off by the beast, flung to rubble), but perhaps, I thought hopefully, there'd been shelter and warmth enough for whichever unlucky souls stood guard here. Back in the warmth of the car, hair still settling down, we made our way to the castle we could see so clearly across the valley – Château de Peyrepertuse – from the one we'd just visited.

It had an entirely different personality: more brutal, less dreamy, rugged and tough and menacingly beautiful.

And on we went. This is how we spent the first few glorious days of our trip, castle-hopping. We were staying in an Airbnb that overlooked the breathtaking medieval citadel of Carcassonne, which in the evening grew warm and alive with lights. We'd drift magnetically towards them, ascending through the purple dusk its winding cobbled walkways until we stepped inside beneath a yawning archway. We sat outside to eat in courtyards almost too perfect, like movie sets, and drank great orbs of red wine until the lamps blurred like stars.

It must've been on the third or fourth morning that we got in the car on our way to see the Pont du Gard, an ancient Roman aqueduct composed of soft yellow sandstone stacked into three rows of semicircles – the top row diddy and those beneath it great yawning things. Like the water it carried centuries ago – cradled, really – down a virtually imperceptible 2.5-centimetre descent towards the Roman colony of Nemausus (Nîmes), 50 kilometres away (a sloping gradient of only 1 in 18,241 across that *entire* journey), we got there eventually.

I say eventually because our journey was not so smooth. No, before we got there we'd screech down roads squiggling off our pre-mapped route on a detour to hell.

We'd just stopped off at a run-down but charming petrol station to pick up some snacks and to have a wee in some very questionable wood-panelled loos for which there was, bafflingly given our remoteness, a snaking queue. Buckled back in and on the road again, Tom or Kate, I can't remember which (probably Kate, Tom was driving), twisted round in their seat to offer me and Jovan some Mentos from a big crinkling bag they'd just bought. I absentmindedly took one with a 'thanks', popped it into my mouth as I was watching bleached fields fly past, and with a crunch felt the unmistakable fast-spreading white-noise tingle of, oh no, time slowing to a treacly, suffocating drawl. Like a child who has fallen and whose low bawl escalates before, one suspects, the pain has even registered, I felt the loose *thing* in my mouth with my tongue before I felt any pain.

My eyes flew wide like a doe in headlights, time slammed into me like a brick wall, and a chanting whisper of 'oh my God, oh my God, oh my God' prompted Jovan to ask me what was up, realisation dawning in his eyes. He was gentle, calm, knowing me better than I knew myself and aware from the off that I was gearing up to lose it completely. He took my hand in his big bear hands and squeezed. 'My tooth's come out,' I said. 'Well, off, my tooth's come off.'

My breathing thinned as I slid into panic. I held the off-white porcelain nugget in my hand and looked down at it, then up at Jovan, then down at it in disbelief. I thought, and not by any means in a straight line, my mind at this point better resembling a BMX flying down a bumpy hill through the woods, *I'm in a foreign country, miles away from my dentist, I can feel the cool air rippling over the thin membrane separating my tooth's already jittery, now jumping and leaping, nerve from the scream of this world and we've got four days of holiday left.*

I want to say it hurt more, to justify my spiralling. The way I heave-cried-breathe-cried would suggest utter agony, as would the speed with which Tom and Kate snapped into clear-headed logistics mode to find me a nearby emergency dentist, but honestly, I was more in shock than anything else. It felt as though I'd fallen asleep and woken up in an upside-down, wrong-coloured cacophonous world where this – the thing I'd been so scared of happening ever since Chorizo Slice-gate – was happening, actually happening. I'd let my guard down, I thought irrationally. I had just been getting on with my life, not preparing as I should have been for the horrible shadowy thing always lurking around the corner in my any-minute-now future. Instead of steeling myself, I'd become intoxicated on time – I'd drunk every drop and savoured its sweet taste – instead of watching it always. Raw shreds of thought came together to form malevolent half-sentences that made a seductive case for anxiety, for the always-readiness I'd unknowingly abandoned. I'd fallen asleep at the wheel. It made no sense, of course. Part of me knew this even at the time. If I could foresee such events, would it make them any easier when they came around? Absofuckinglutely not, obviously; I'd live a life paralysed by fear. But was that not what was happening already? I felt in a bind and scared and trapped and I couldn't stop probing the raw tooth with my tongue.

Tooth

In N.K. Jemisin's epic *Broken Earth* trilogy, the earth is a living creature hell-bent on vengeance after greedy humans tried to drain it of life. In pursuit of revenge, it has flung its only child, the moon, hurtling through space. It does everything to shiver people off its surface once and for all, creating seasons that choke the air with ash, tsunamis and earthquakes, killing millions. Anyway, it doesn't matter whether you've read the books (which, oh my God, you *should*), just that you know there are these characters called Guardians who have a metal chip made of the earth lodged deep in the base of their skulls, which exerts the evil earth's sentient, malevolent will over them and whispers things like, 'Hello, little enemy.'

As the years flew away from that horrible time in the dentist's chair where I had my permanent crown fitted, I began to forget it was even there. That is, until every few months or so I would wake up and feel a flutter beneath the surface of the tooth, a glimmer of something shivering awake. In my head that's how I'd refer to it, talk to it almost like it was a sentient being too. *Hello, little enemy. You're awake, are you?* In some grim way I imagined it like a pregnancy, like the twinge kicks to my stomach telling me *I'm alive* and *I'm awake*. I've not been pregnant yet – one day I'd like to be – but I wonder when mams feel those kicks whether they do occasionally feel a shudder of anxiety knowing the crisis of childbirth is up ahead like a portent. These little twangs in my lower right jaw felt portentous to me, like reminders that a moment of calamity was only ever round the corner. The ramifications felt so much darker, so much scarier, than *just* a trip to the dentist. And the Oxford English Dictionary does list one of its definitions of 'pregnant' as 'destined to produce a great many results or consequences, fraught *with*; (also) full of significance, momentous,' so maybe I'm not entirely mental.

I thought about all these things and more as we sped to wherever Google Maps was taking us. *Why did you have to wake up?* my inner voice asked my little enemy, *and why here?* In what must have been less than an hour – not so long as to wipe me out entirely but long enough for me to stop whimpering – the car pulled into an empty parking lot next to a blank building that looked like nothing. We tentatively entered, walking up a blank corridor to knock on a door that apparently belonged to a private dentist. No response. After a few more knocks, the door opposite it, on the other side of the hall, opened, and a woman wearing (thank the lord) what looked like scrubs popped her head out. She looked completely bewildered, which, fair. In a flurry of French, Kate, who would later laugh that she didn't think her French quite extended to dental emergencies, ascertained that the dentist was not here. The lovely nurse did give us an address, though, and back to the car we went.

Eventually, we walked into what was very discernibly a dentist's waiting room. Language barrier aside, there was no arguing with glossy posters of gummy white smiles plastering the walls, nor the sterile smell of plastic-covered chairs. Kate was magnificent. Flanked by a shy-looking nurse/dentist/receptionist, she handed me a clipboard, and I couldn't help but smile as together they spoke and acted out what each section meant (for the section on allergies, the woman mimed a sneeze, and we got there laughing and smiling in the end).

Sadly, no amount of charades and loveliness could dull the eventual horror of sitting on a dentist's chair while surgically masked people speak in a language you don't understand while coming ever closer to your face with what sounds like a buzz saw. In the end I squeezed my eyes shut and didn't feel a thing beyond the sharp rush of streaming cold air they blew onto the tooth with a little metal utensil, and them pressing down on the crown (which had up until this point been clutched firmly in my sweaty Gollum fist) until the glue or cement or whatever was sufficiently set to send me on my way.

After we'd paid, we got back into the car, resuming our journey to the aqueduct having only lost two or so hours in all. As soon as my head hit Jovan's shoulder, I was out like a light. The rest of the day is a teary blur, though my memories of it are warm and happy and excited. The place was incredible and, knowing acutely that I was at risk of wasting a once in a lifetime experience by worrying, I tried really hard to appreciate it, to learn all about the history of the place and make sensory memories that bottled the way the hot, humid air felt on my skin, the way the view expanded in all directions, the way lunch tasted. It's still cut through with a sharp, bitter taste, though. If the day were rock strata, there would be a thin, hard, gritty line in an otherwise big expanse of cream and white.

That evening I ate soup. I vowed only to eat soup ever again, but this lasted fewer than twelve hours. I spent a lot of time back at our Airbnb, once again staring at the innocuous-looking thing in the bathroom mirror. I was overwhelmed with a desire to test out the glue, to prod the crown to see if it moved, to hook my nail under the groove I'd already identified with my tongue to see if it would just ping off. I pressed down hard on the smooth surface, which dips in the middle and then up again, until I'd woken it up. I weirdly wanted to know if it, whatever *it* was, was still there. *I am*, came the reply.

In the days and weeks after, I did this compulsively: looking at it, testing its strength, slipping into panic if I spotted what I thought was a new groove or inconsistency, then slipping out again. Long weeks were intermittently rent open by a piercing twinge that thrust my mind back into a heightened alertness. Exhaustion would slowly zone me out of these states as though dipping between radio stations. The gaps in the static have got longer and longer, and I can go months without thinking about that tooth. But every now and again, most often when I'm least expecting it, it wakes up.

8
Walnut

The word 'diagnosis' is a funny one. It stems from the Greek word *diagnōsis* (makes sense), which itself apparently stems from the longer *diagignōskein*, not an Icelandic metal band but a word which means to 'discern, distinguish' – literally, 'to know thoroughly' or 'know apart'. *Dia*, I gather, means 'between', while *gignōskein*, 'to learn, to come to know', comes from the root *gno*: 'to know'.

But it's easier to dissect a word than the brain. Figuratively speaking, that is. I'm sure in a literal sense it's just like slicing into pigs' livers in biology class. Effortless, like butter. But that's what makes it so weird! We know so little, really, about the secret work this meaty slab does, what the most elusive, powerful blobfish-looking *thing* in the entire universe gets up to in its spare time; capable not only of perceiving that vast, boundless universe but of holding infinite universes inside itself, of inventing new ones. More complicated still is the brain's relentless movement. I don't mean this literally, though it does put me in mind of when the Holy Rosary headteacher Mr Lyons told us that on hot days our brains would physically shrink if we didn't drink enough water, and I imagined my tiny walnut brain rattling around up there as I starved myself of wee-producing liquids. I mean, it's not the same brain day to day – it's forging crackling new connections daily, hourly, secondly, overwriting again and again what's gone before; rewriting memories, then memories of memories. It's more ocean than solid ground, its wibbly wet grooves and undulations, folds and turns, hiding so much even from itself.

Taking this into account, it's a marvel we're so tied to the notion of a single self, and that said self should be consistent over time. Encased in just the one body, just one brain, we've tied our selfhood to these things as if they really were themselves static entities. But it's not as though that body is just the one body, really. My once-tight little body relaxing into childbearing hips and a gait that would increasingly make Jemima Puddle-Duck jealous tells me that much. I suppose if we all treated each other like the impossible aliens we are to one another, inhabiting the chasmic space between even the simplest of words and fully perceiving the depths of one another, we would get nothing done. Or we'd fall irresistibly in love and start a sexually experimental global cult. In any case, it seems the wheels of society need us to skim this ocean's surface to keep on turning (Is it a swan-shaped plastic paddle boat? Am I talking about propellers? Time to step away from the abyss I think). I say this, by the way, as a non-expert non-anthropologist non-professional here. Sorry if the above scientifically rigorous explanation gave you the wrong impression. Yes, 'wibbly' is a medical term.

Walnut

Diagnosing mental illnesses and disorders relies at least initially on observable surface realities: behaviours. If there's a giant squid under the ship, it'll make the ship do some things its crew weren't expecting. (It's strange, isn't it, how we blame the ship rather than the squid?) Unfortunately for me, my GP cannot open up my bonce and peer around with a torch to find out what's festering where. Indeed, she would likely go completely insane before she'd even reached the good stuff. Instead, she can gauge through talking to me and through questionnaires the ways in which my mental anguish is expressing itself on the outside.

Am I sleeping a lot or too little? Over- or under-eating? Information gathered, she can of course try and tinker with the insides, but the opacity of the whole brain thing requires a process of trial and error until I finally, hopefully, find something that obsequiously pulls the right internal strings (*you're just such a lovely brain, honestly one of the best, it's such an honour to be represented by you and I really hope we can continue to improve our working – OK I know it hasn't really been working – relationship*) to coax it into releasing a bit more happy juice like a fat cat holding the purse strings. Before that point, though, my brain will likely (has) reject some of the silver-plattered delicacies I've, on my knees like a palace slave, humbly offered it. The tantrum it pulls when it doesn't like what it sees can make one less and less likely to try again. Both the brain and me, well, we get exhausted by the effort.

To be Captain Obvious for a moment, hitting on the right thing, though, can be lifesaving. Enough people displaying a similar set of behaviours has helped medical professionals distinguish (or diagnose, if the definition 'distinctive characterisation in precise terms' is applied) common (in the sense of shared, not necessarily regular) underlying pathologies that bring us closer and closer to making sense of the pesky brain. It's not as though every doctor is going in fully blind every time, and there are certain drugs that generally help ameliorate certain illnesses. It's a crude and imperfect art and doesn't work the same way person to person, but it's something.

My GP (a shapeshifting figure of which there have been many) has never done a proper assessment of me, or at least not that I can remember. For me, trying to get to the bottom of whatever has always twisted inside me, albeit in different ways, has been nearly as emotionally difficult as actually living with whatever *it* is.

My first encounter with a counsellor was when I was 15, in the GP surgery to the left of the college field that incorporated the one we'd always gone to at the end of the long arterial road Ashleigh once lived on. That one had just been a house turned into a doctor's office, but this new building was all glass and polished pine, and as I waited I felt optimistic and nervous all at once. When my name finally scrolled hesitantly across the red LED sign, I walked to the small room and plonked down in a seat opposite a white-haired man with a wide face and smiling eyes. I'd been struggling with anger, then, he asked. In fits of upset at my mam and myself and the world, I'd taken to sweeping everything off the top of chests of drawers, sending powders and dried-up mascaras to the floor, as well as vases that occasionally would not shatter. When they did, I was always surprised at myself, but being in a blind rage made me feel better in the moment. Exhausted, I'd then slump down in bed and cry until I couldn't breathe. So, we spoke. It must've been for six hour-long sessions or so, and then … that was it.

He'd gone through various imaginative techniques to help reset my mind and prevent outbursts ('Imagine your anger is a balloon. Better to let the air out slowly than to pop it in a big bang'), had empathised with me and told me it would be OK, but then the sessions ran out. I didn't understand. I was still panicking every time someone didn't pick up the phone, worrying they'd died or had decided they didn't love me after all. I was still struggling to contain my emotions. But the six hours were suddenly up and I was politely ushered out with a regretful-sounding 'good luck' and a closed door.

I wouldn't get help again until I was at university, four or five years later. Being away from home alone and for an extended period, I felt like I was falling without end through the brambles near Rose's house. Only it wasn't fun, and I wasn't sure I'd come out the other side. Things that had before seemed OK or normal developed jagged edges puncturing my insides; my mind was flooded with confusion and acidic uncertainty, and I applied to the university's counselling service. After a couple of weeks' wait, I entered a sour-smelling room and sat before a female counsellor who looked tired and vaguely irritated by my presence. She got right down to it, biro poised over a notebook, asking me among her very first questions what my relationship with my dad was like. I explained it was good and I hadn't come to talk about that, my speech becoming thicker and heavier with emotion until my mind was in a spin and, frustrated, I left. I grabbed my coat off the back of the chair and said it didn't matter, stepping out of the warm, stuffy office into chill autumn air. The streaks of tears felt cold on my cheeks, and I walked back to my room angry.

My anxiety reached fever pitch during those three years. After a subsequent, desperate email to the college counsellor revealed a packed schedule with no room in it for me, I nervously booked a GP appointment. When I arrived, I was surprised to have seated in front of me not a GP but two girls who looked around the same age as me. In my frantic need to see someone, fast, I'd hastily yes-ed away the receptionist's enquiry as to whether I'd mind seeing a trainee if it got me an appointment sooner, and here I was.

As my guts spilled onto the scratchy carpet in front of the pair, my racking sobs sending uncomfortable glances shooting from one trainee to the other, their eyes avoiding mine and seeking out each other's, my descriptions of perpetual claustrophobia, trappedness, fear, inability to perform even the most basic functions, desperation, and a sense of self that flickered like a broken projector, they said very little. Sometimes one nodded, took scant notes, which I think was their way of dispelling the anxiety they themselves were feeling sat opposite this unstable black hole of a person throbbing ominously in front of them.

When I'd exhausted myself, eyes tiny as piss-holes in the snow, one of them asked to be excused for one moment. After a few seconds they re-entered with the doctor who I'd been expecting to see at the start and whispered what could've been no more than ten words (not enough, I thought, to capture the lifelong existential dread I'd unfurled in my breathless monologue). The doctor, an older blonde woman, then smiled at me and said, 'We'll start you off on 50 mg of citalopram, OK?' before leaving the office as quickly as she'd entered. I took the prescription to Boots straight away, still feeling like I'd been spun around and around, stunned and confused by what had just happened, and as it was handed to me, hope welled quietly in my chest. I popped the pill as soon as I got back to my room, winter night already falling full-black, and getting into bed fully dressed, I propped my massive HP laptop up onto my tits to watch *The Office* (US, obviously) again. After two or three hours I started to feel very, *very* weird.

It was like a switch had been flicked; panic was suddenly rising in my chest, and I could feel my heart racing louder than my overheating laptop's fan. It wasn't even the 'Michael's Proposal' episode or 'Jim and Pam's Wedding', so I knew it couldn't be that, and, frightened, I stepped out into the hallway and entered the shared bathroom where there was a mirror. The blinking light metallically clanked on and I nearly screamed when I saw my reflection. My pupils were round and wide as the moon, inky black and huge. My hands were starting to shake and I felt like I was being unwillingly pulled outside of my body, like I was drifting away. I was struck by an urgent certainty that if I couldn't get back into it soon, I'd never be able to. *I'm disappearing. I'm disappearing and there's nothing I can do about it.* Next minute I was standing in the centre of my square, sparsely decorated room. Just standing there, feeling the world shift beneath my feet like jelly.

One of my best friends, Charlotte, lived in the room right beneath mine, and I'd told her I'd started taking an SSRI (Selective Serotonin Reuptake Inhibitor) and if I started feeling weird could I knock on her door? Of course, I could, any time. But I was so heartbreakingly anxious at that time that I couldn't settle comfortably into a conversation with any of my friends, my self-awareness a screaming kettle that made me paranoid and intense. I watched myself trying to talk like a normal person, but what came out was often weird or unintentionally rude or harsh. I acted out, overconfident one minute and silent the next. I felt trapped behind a mask, and though my small group were lovely and, I realise now, loved me all the same, I felt increasingly alienated, convinced I had no friends, that they didn't like me, and more and more like I was a broken person being futilely held up like a disjointed marionette for them to examine.

So on that occasion I didn't go downstairs for a cup of fruit tea. My feet were for now firmly planted like tree trunks into the middle of my square, barren room, my mind on fire, being pulled in all directions like that poor doomed victim of *The Bacchae*, torn limb from limb.

I stopped taking the tablets after four days. The trainees had told me they might take up to four weeks to start settling in, and they had warned me there'd be side effects. Nausea and headaches I could deal with; a hallucinatory sense I was disappearing, coming on like clockwork two hours after I'd taken the stupid things, I could not. I'd love to say I went back to the GP to try something new, to try to find a better fit, but I was terrified. Instead, I got up every day and played the part of a person, until eventually my costume started to fit again.

Then I moved to Wales to do a Master's and outgrew the costume. Twenty-two and still crushed by the imagined weight of an uncertain future, sad and unsure of myself or, well, anything, and clinging onto Institutionalised Life where I knew the rules and felt safe, like a baby refusing to leave a warm, comfy womb, I tried again. Desperate to quieten the noise constantly, relentlessly, buzzing in my head, I registered for a GP and found myself once again erupting in tears in front of a frazzled middle-aged woman who waited patiently for my life story to end.

'I feel wrong, people don't seem to understand but I just *know* something is wrong with me,' I opined. 'But nobody will tell me what is wrong they just give me tablets but they didn't work this time but maybe a different kind will work this time I don't know I think I'm willing to try something if you think it might help me, I'm sure I've got anxiety and depression that has to be it, I can't imagine what else it could be, unless you think maybe it's something else? It's just that I'm always crying and down and not sleeping then sleeping too much and I can't concentrate and I don't see the point in anything or in me when I'm such a burden on everyone and anyway depression runs in my family my mam has it so it must be that, right, so if you could please tell me what is wrong then maybe I can try and fix it.'

She took a deep, impatient-sounding breath and said we could try sertraline, which often agreed with people better than citalopram (I don't know if this is true). 'But wait, can we at least try and diagnose me with something [tears are pooling in my eyes again] before we try and medicate it? Surely you need to know what is wrong before you know what tablets to prescribe? I know SSRIs are usually used for anxiety and depression, so would you say that's what you're treating? [She's telling me to try and calm down because I need to be calm for her to help me] I'm not trying to be aggressive I've just been trying to get help for years and years and no one seems to understand and it's like no one can hear me when I'm saying I need help.'

'We can put anxiety and depression on your medical record if it will make you feel better,' she said, and so she did. I walked back to the house I lived in with strangers, completely numb, and went straight to bed. My brain, I think, went into survival mode, completely overwhelmed to the point it had to shut down for a bit. I lived on the ground floor, my bay window facing the street where passing strangers peered in, so the curtains were conveniently already closed. I missed home, missed hearing Liv coming up and down the stairs, missed the distant hum of the TV I'd know Mam was watching, missed being surrounded by people who loved me. Instead, outside my room were the footsteps of people I barely knew, and inside those four walls I questioned who I was, deconstructing myself, tearing my walls – already crumbling – down, scrabbling for a personhood to anchor myself to.

A couple of days later, feeling slightly more rested, feeling slightly more like a person again, I went and picked up my sertraline. Within a couple of hours of taking my first one, I had a foggy headache and couldn't stop yawning, but I was still attached to myself. No severance seemed to have occurred, the string attaching me to me – however frayed – intact, and I hesitatingly let myself think that maybe they would work this time. For the first two weeks I felt sick and tired and foggy, a bit fluey, all in all. But I was still here, so this time I plugged on. I'd been given a leaflet by the doctor (by this point in the appointment, as I was logging off for the day, I heard her talk from very, very far away) and she'd explained talking therapy as well as medication would give me the best chance.

So, I once again dabbled with the student service, which she said would work best for me because I was a student.

I felt patronised by her and got the sense she saw a lot of students in her surgery and thought we all ought to toughen up a bit. Once again, I found myself sitting across from a man smiling an over-sympathetic, tight-lipped smile.

I was clenching my jaw really badly that day. The leaflet that came with my prescription explained that it was a side effect, but I didn't expect it to happen to me. My skull felt like it had been screwed together too tight. Passers-by on the street probably thought I was on MDMA given the size of my pupils (not as huge as last time but still obsidian pools) and how much I was gurning, twitching. Sometimes my teeth chattered uncontrollably like I was cold. I wasn't.

This guy was younger than most of the people I'd seen so far (apart from the two students). He was a bit unkempt but in a 'cool young dad' kind of way, tattooed and relaxed, and he explained apologetically that this wasn't a counselling session but a session to determine what kind of counselling I might need and whether they might be able to provide it given the long waiting lists they were experiencing.

'What do you think might help?' he asked gently.

'Well, I don't know,' I said. 'No one has told me what's wrong with me.'

'Huh,' he said, knowingly, but without explaining to me why he was reacting that way, and he asked me to explain what had been going on with me up to this point. How I'd got here. I gave him a potted history, obviously crying again, right up until the GP appointment and the sertraline they'd prescribed me two weeks ago. As soon as I stopped talking, I tried very hard to keep my jaw still. I don't know if he noticed.

What happened next still floors me. A beat, and this dude started polemicising on the evils of Big Pharma and how GPs are giving out SSRIs like bandages or candy and that it's a disgusting indictment of the state of the NHS and society that so many millions of people are on them. Looking back now, I soften a bit because he seemed to be a genuinely kind guy who wanted to help people, and he made some very valid points. But I'd just got further than I'd ever got into a course of treatment, after having made the very difficult and, I thought quietly, brave decision to try something that might help me again after a terrifying experience with it before. My jaw was hurting. I was zoning out again, going up and far away from here, filling out forms with hands that weren't mine, smiling and hearing myself say 'bye' to him as he saw me out. I felt floored. I went straight home to bed, falling asleep to the warring cacophony of *should I stop or nots* in my tired, pressurised head.

I kept taking the sertraline, swallowing my sickness and waiting for a miracle. One morning I woke up and did feel different. Not miraculously so, and I didn't notice it right away. But when I sat on the beige, cracked-leather couch by the window overlooking the overgrown garden that morning, my mouthful of Weetabix was suddenly delicious. I thought, like a cartoon character in my head,

Wow, that's absolutely lovely. I laughed at myself, but it was true. And outside the sun seemed to be shining brighter than usual, and there were chirping birds zipping across the fences. Some blockage seemed to have been removed and my brain felt full of fresh air, like someone had opened a window. Then something remarkable happened. I had a day where I didn't think about myself or who I was or how I was acting or what I was saying or whether the medication was working. I laughed with my friends and attended lectures I was able to focus on, even enjoy.

Not all days were like this thereafter, I was disappointed to discover. I stopped noticing the exquisite taste of Weetabix, or watching the birds like a drugged-up Snow White. But I did start going for short runs – when I hadn't seen the point before – and managing full nights of sleep. I kept taking the tablets but didn't get any counselling. I'd emailed the guy and told him how he'd made me feel and I could tell he was genuinely very sorry, but the whole thing felt soured, and anyway, I was doing great!

My exams finished on a Friday and, having panicked and accepted the first job I was offered, I moved my life to London the following Monday. I hadn't seen the house or met the people living there, but the Rightmove ad seemed fine and my boyfriend's mam had scoped them out for me: 'They seem nice, but the room you'd be staying in is quite small.' I didn't want the anxiety of looking for a place, the uncertainty and stress that doing something slowly would bring. Likewise, the job hunt. I just wanted one, because then I knew I was not going to fall between the cracks I was imagining. Being in-between was for me the worst possible scenario. I'd experienced the horror of having the rug pulled out from under me, emerging into an uncertain world after graduating, and I wasn't going to let that happen again. I was strong, independent, resilient. I could live anywhere and make it work.

When I arrived, the couple seemed like deer in headlights, as though they hadn't been aware that I was moving into their house – wary of me, almost. They were about thirty, attractive, normal-seeming, and we exchanged pleasantries as my bags pooled around my feet on the threshold. They told me which room was mine and I went upstairs to see it.

There used to be a programme on the BBC where parents would cede full creative control of their house to their kids, who would then design a makeover for it that nine times out of ten would make the parents nearly faint. I can't remember there ever being any incentive, financial or otherwise, so why they would let their maniacal cartoon-crazed kids go wild I do not know. But the designs were just magnificent. Replace the stairs with a slide (I loved this one, since it was one thing for kids to slide down and scramble back up the way they came, another for adults trying to get ready for work to scramble on all fours 'upstairs'); turn the kitchen into a fully functional industrial McDonald's kitchen complete with yellow and red dining area; secret hideaways through hidden doors; wacky colours; gumball machines; and inflatable furniture. One kid, clearly not feeling The Muse that day, just had the outside of the house (front, back and sides) painted with a St George's cross.

My room in London might reasonably have slotted into this miscellaneous category of imaginative, futuristic design as it took the concept of the 'bedroom' to its most literal conclusion. You see, it wasn't just a room with a bed in it, it was a room made up entirely of bed. A not-quite-a-double bed, to be precise. Who among us hasn't thought at least once how bloody comfortable and cool it would be to have a room that was literally all bed, a *bed room*, a wall-to-wall, corner-to-corner mattress floor? Sure, that Louis Theroux episode about swingers had sullied the concept for me somewhat, in that the *bed room* was a waterproof-sheet-fitted reality of nightmarish proportions (there was scuba fetishwear on the walls, something my London box room sadly lacked). But here I was, living the dream.

There was so little floor space to manoeuvre around, in fact, that one winter evening as I attempted to exit the room I accidentally sat in a bowl of pasta bake that I'd been eating alone in bed. It burned my bum a bit and I swore, taking the cheese-and-tomato-sauced culottes off and changing into my pyjamas early. When I got back into the room, I ate my bum pasta and didn't think of it again. That is, until I went to work the next day. Anyone who suffers from depression and anxiety will understand that tasks such as laundry can feel like Herculean feats of will and strength, and doing such tasks in a houseful of strangers who seem suspicious of you and irritated by your presence is even less desirable. I stayed in my room as much as possible, avoiding the annoyed glances of my housemates (who, it was clear, wanted to live as a couple in their own house but couldn't afford the London prices. I was, I think, a symbol of their understandable resentment). So I was, I'm not proud to say, re-wearing clothes. Especially my black New Look culottes, which went with every outfit and which I could shove on without thinking.

I'd got up from my desk to get some tea when one of the girls said I had something on the back of my trousers. Not for the first time, I went cold as the realisation ran through me. 'Oh God, what the hell?' I pretended. 'I must've sat in something horrible on the train this morning. Ugh, how disgusting!' Emily, one of my wonderful colleagues, was a warm ray of pure sunshine in my life at that time, looking after me in a way that said without saying, 'I understand, and I've got you.' Going to work every day felt like coming home, and going 'home' felt like going to work. Intuiting that I was embarrassed, she came with me in the lift down to the ground floor where there were showers for staff members to use. No one else in there, the morning gym rush mercifully over, I stepped out of my trousers and – now clad in blouse and knickers and socks only – scrubbed at my trousers in the sink with hand soap and water. Emily stayed with me, never once making me feel embarrassed, my London sister watching me furiously scrub pasta bake off the bum of my trousers in our work toilets, fighting back tears and wanting to go home.

My other colleagues had wondered how on earth I could have sat in something clearly so wet and chunky on the train without realising, without feeling it seeping through to my pants. I laughed with them, screaming inside, but Emily didn't ask as I held the wet, now-bobbly patch of fabric under the hand dryer with one eye on the door in case I'd be caught with my pants down. I didn't ever admit the truth of the situation to Emily or anyone else, went about the rest of my day subdued and feeling down, but I wonder whether a scent of pomodoro wafted over to Emily as the dryer did God's work that day.

The shared bathroom in the house was almost as small as the closet in which I lived. When I first walked in, I gasped in horror. The light wasn't operated by a switch but the kind of rope pulley Mam had at home, hanging down from the ceiling and making a satisfying noise when activated. However, instead of the tasteful, ornamental handle I was used to, this string was tied around the neck of a blue cartoonish character with 'X's for eyes. Every time you pulled the string to turn the light on, or (ominously, given the circumstances) off, you hanged him anew. Since I already felt about as at home in the house as a virus in a body, such homely touches didn't make me feel any more at ease. In the WhatsApp group that included me, the couple, and a 40-or-so-year-old Canadian woman who worked for the local council and lived in the room next to mine, I plucked up the courage to say it made me uncomfortable and that it was distasteful and weird, that there'd been suicide in my family, and they reluctantly cut him down. I was expected to replace it, I knew, but I didn't. I barely had the money to cover rent, travel to and from work, sustenance. So the fraying string hung limply mid-air and I was not forgiven.

The pair didn't want me to use the house like it was mine as much as theirs, despite the big flush of cash I sent them monthly suggesting otherwise. I felt like a child who'd been foisted onto unwilling distant relatives who had no choice but to begrudgingly take me in. Don't get me wrong, I understood that they'd lived there for years and had a way of doing things. But the living room, for example, was entirely theirs, and even though they said I could use it whenever I wanted, I soon learnt by the way they awkwardly looked at me and spoke to me that I shouldn't watch TV there. Voluntarily or involuntarily, they denied me the human contact I so desperately craved. I was lonely, dreading leaving work every day to a house whose sounds belonged to complete strangers – people who didn't care about me or even know me. During those months, I thought a lot about the lessons we'd been taught as kids – don't get into cars with strangers, don't talk to strangers – yet here I was, sleeping mere steps away from them, like so many millions of others. I was living in a spare room and I felt like a spare person.

My boyfriend came to stay one weekend soon after I first moved in, and I was elated to feel the house flood with colour and hear the sounds of someone who loved me, brushing his teeth in the bathroom and breathing beside me in his sleep. I felt revived when he left, like I'd just eaten a big, delicious meal, but not long after he'd gone someone knocked on my door.

'Can I have a word?'

The Irish woman's tones were clipped and, as she was standing on the threshold to my room, presented no option but for me to nervously say, 'Yes.' So I said, 'Yes, of course, what's up?'

'You didn't ask us if it was OK for your boyfriend to stay?'

I was flabbergasted. My jaw dropped. What to say to that? Momentarily frozen, I thawed to respond, 'I didn't realise I had to ask permission … He's my boyfriend and, since I live here now, will be coming to visit me here every other weekend or so. Is that a problem?' I was starting to think I'd completely misread the entire situation, that I was an idiot who didn't understand how living with strangers was supposed to work because no one had ever taught me the appropriate etiquette, and I was just trying to not scream how lonely I was out the window and here, now, in her stony face. Had I really misstepped so badly? So unknowingly? Was I really so ill-equipped to read a social situation? I was being put in my place and alongside confoundment I was angry and second-guessing myself, turning over and over in my mind what I thought I knew and how I could've got it so wrong.

'This is a four-person house and we like to keep it that way. We don't want other people staying here.'

They'd been so lovely and welcoming to him, in a way which honestly shocked me, when I'd introduced him. It was like they were completely different people, but I felt a modicum of relief. Maybe they weren't so bad after all, maybe I'd been paranoid and on edge having just moved so quickly to a big city and hadn't I, after all, been welcomed into their home?

All that was shattered. Whenever I went to hang my dripping clothes on the clothes horse, I felt their eyes trail me across the room. I was paranoid, no doubt, but hostility ran through the brickwork and I felt lost and alone. I'd take walks around the unfamiliar neighbourhood, just to get away for a while. I reassured myself like a child that I'd made the right decision, I was OK, I didn't need (as my heart so often told me) to go home. I luxuriated in my family's northern tones over the phone, as warming as hot tomato soup, and swallowed back tears as I told them how well I was doing; I knew they worried.

And it was here that I started picking my skin for half-hours at a time, belly lumped over the small sink, the door locked behind me and the light string swaying, unweighted. I felt a sense of safety, peace, escape. I wish I could tell you what spurred it on – maybe there was one particular imperfection that started the snowball – but no, I just remember the mirror, flecked; the fraying string that turned on the bright, pore-illuminating light, and the sense of escape I felt being in there, absorbed in a task that took me somewhere else.

Despite all this, believing myself better, I stopped taking my antidepressants. Out of nowhere really. I should've known my inability to walk the thirty seconds to the mini pharmacy on the corner was an obvious sign not to do so. But I felt, despite my loneliness and anxiety, more mentally stable than I had in a very long time. I was aware of the things that were bothering me and could manage them, I thought. I think now, though, that I'd forgotten to renew my prescription and after a week off them decided I was, wow, fine – that I didn't need them like I thought I did. After about ten days without them, I started getting 'brain zaps' at work, a metallic rush like shoals of shimmering fish flooding my brain, replaced in a flash by a deep, expectant blue still quivering from their movement. I'd feel woozy immediately afterwards, sway unnoticeably on my feet as though hit by a blast of icy wind if I was standing up (on my way back from the tea station, most likely) but other than that I felt fine.

That is, until I didn't. As the depressed, anxious brain is wont to do, I attributed my sudden descent to existential matters of self and worth and nothing to do with the fact I'd come off the tablets that had stabilised me. A trip to my GP saw me referred to a course on 'overcoming worry'. Being off antidepressants had become a sort of test of personal will, a battle with myself to see how long

I could go without. *They were making you fat, anyway*, I'd tell myself, conveniently ignoring the staggering absence of physical activity in my life and the pasta-bum-bakes I ate every night, slathered in bubbling cheese. It was a way, ironically, of taking the reins of my life. My new, independent life. Or so I thought.

By this time, I'd escaped the mad house, by the way. I couldn't take it any more; I was sure I was going to end up six feet under their back garden the next time I had the audacity to invite a friend over for dinner. I thought everything would change when I moved into a flat with friends. Or, rather, a university acquaintance with whom I was friendly but not close, and a friend of a friend who was very sweet but, again, who I didn't really know. But I didn't care. I wanted out, and out I got.

The new flat looked like a crime scene when we arrived. It sat on the corner of Uxbridge Road, right across from Shepherd's Bush Green. Relentless traffic rattled the windows in their frames, off-white walls were smeared with dark, unidentifiable blurs, mattresses were marked and worn, abandoned personal items from the previous tenants hung on the coat pegs. The carpeted hallway stairs smelled like stale urine. I took the smallest room, trying to be nice, just so grateful to be here. But it was the Wrong Choice. Both tall windows faced the main road, and black soot, presumably from pollution, gathered in their corners. The blinds were broken and I'd have to wait to get new ones. I got dressed in the bathroom since the whole world could see in. *Don't cry*, I told myself. *It's going to be better here.*

The windows were thin and draughty, and for the first month I couldn't sleep because it was so bright and loud. So loud I felt like there were no windows at all, like I was just sleeping on top of the burger restaurant below, exposed to the elements and passing eyes. All my furniture was still there, on that roof: my bed, my cheap clothes rack that collapsed every other day, but just no walls. Like a sad piece of performance art. A mouse ducked and dived between the gaps beneath the kitchen cabinets. We couldn't fit more than one of us at a time in the kitchen, and without a living room we turned the spare room (cupboard is a more appropriate descriptor; the bloodsucking landlord clearly hadn't been able to squeeze a single bed in there) into something of a social space.

Beanbags were bought from Argos, cheap art from Flying Tiger. Dad came to visit, and later he told me his stomach had dropped when he saw the place. I couldn't blame him. But hey, we were a stone's throw away from two tube stations, a Wetherspoons, a McDonald's and Westfield Shopping Centre. What more could I want? Sure, I watched as police wrestled a man to the ground right beneath my window, and was certain, increasingly paranoid, that I was being followed home on several occasions (once, a man jumped out from behind a car as I walked to my front door and shouted 'Good morrow!' at me like some kind of highway bandit), but I had made a fresh start, three or four months since moving into the Irish couple's house. I could do this. After all, my budget was slim even by non-London prices, and after plugging that modest monthly sum into housing websites, I was presented with cursed rooms with twin beds in them, aghast to find on scrolling that I'd be getting for my cash just one of the beds and sleeping next to a complete stranger. The number of listings that specified 'females only' – not women, females – sent a shiver right through me. One search result showed a picture of a concrete kerb sprung with weeds. Confused, I clicked on the link and discovered that for my budget I could get a 'prime car-parking space', Monday through Friday. With a grim chuckle I imagined myself lying in the foetal position, asleep on it. *It could be worse*, I said to myself constantly. *It could be worse, and this is all OK.*

But I was lying to myself. I didn't want to 'fail at London', to let everyone down (Who? I didn't know). But I was furious at the world, more blood-boiling angry and confused and embittered than I had any right to be as a privileged graduate, feeling like everything was just completely fucked and bad things happened to good people and everything was just so unfair in this hellhole – it made me sick. I had no money, my brain was zap-zapping, and I felt the familiar swell of claustrophobic panic rising in my chest like floodwaters. *No*, I thought. *Please, no. This was meant to be different. Please, please.* It wasn't only the previous house that had made me feel like a virus it was desperately trying to expel, I realised.

London was like that too, its huge roiling body trying to rid itself of me like a toxin. I was being squeezed out.

I went to the bathroom, the new bathroom, which was longer if not wider than the couple's, and heaved myself over the sink to get myself as close as possible to the mirror. I wanted to see every single pore as wide and big as possible, to squeeze every single one on my face until I felt calm again. Time here would slip by unnoticed. I forgot myself, forgot where I was and why, and forgot all those questions tangling like barbed wire, snagging on my brain. I spoke to myself of 'yield', as if this really were some excavation project for which I was team leader.

Afterwards, when I'd either snapped out of my trance-like state myself or a rap on the bathroom door told me I'd been in too long, I'd think *that was a good yield*. As in, I managed to squeeze out stuff, not just blood pooling because of broken skin, but actual spot-stuff. It felt, in a twisted sort of way, like an achievement. If the sebum or pus or whatever was there, that surely meant it needed to come out. That it was there to be plundered and I'd plundered it, corrected it, set it aright. I felt like I was doing something good for myself, something cleansing, almost like I was squeezing out my thoughts themselves, toxins that needed to be expelled. Of course, the act just bred more spots, a higher yield. I didn't mind; by then I was hooked. At work I'd unconsciously trail a finger around my hairline, under my jaw, silently rejoicing when I felt a bump. I'd gleefully look forward to getting home and picking it, a treat to anticipate and to pull me through the day. None of this seemed odd to me. It was harmless and everyone picked their spots, right? So it didn't even occur to me that this was the first stirrings of a monster. Eventually, I couldn't wait until I got home and would slink off to the work toilets. I'd be irrationally angry if someone else came into the toilets and caught me. I'd pretend I was just sorting out my fringe and would try again soon. I levitated on these moments of respite, untouchable, I thought, finally calm.

It's paradoxical, then, that I knew how not-calm I was. The picking was like a whole chunk of my life that I just ignored as having no actual bearing on anything else. Despite falling asleep remembering the perfect spots I'd picked, the ones that had really ruptured and flew, I thought nothing of the habit. Loneliness and displacement continued to shatter me, and it was for this sense of impending doom and the sense again that I was disappearing that I sought help from my GP. I didn't mention the picking during our appointment – I didn't even think of it.

So, I attended this 'overcoming worry' course. Luckily it was only down the road from the office in Twickenham where I worked, and my teammates were lovely about letting me go during work hours – the only times available. I walked to the ramshackle building feeling hopeful, energised by the possibility of change, and while sitting in the bleak, beige sitting room I smiled widely, warmly, at anyone who caught my eye. *It's OK*, I wanted to say, *we're here now and we're going to be alright.* We came in all shapes and sizes, some with sad eyes, some with happy expressions, some with postures bent and others slickly suited and shuffling where they sat, uncomfortable, perhaps, to be surrounded by such weariness and regretting they'd come.

Eventually, we were herded into an equally bleak room lined this time with worn plastic seats before a flipchart. Two smiley young presenters – for that's how they came across to me, like CBBC presenters or Butlin's redcoats – welcomed us all. They had marker pens poised in their hands. All seated, they began their routine, first outlining what 'worry' was using volunteered words on the first page of the flipchart. The woman's writing was bubbly and large. I tried to remain patient, to not let the minutes as they rolled by confirm the irritation stirring in my belly. It felt like a primary school class, like we were being condescended to in thick saccharine tones. *I know what worry is*, I wanted to scream. *I'm the motherfucking expert and I bet you these people all are too.* The hour was a bust and I stormed back to the office ready to never go again.

The next week, I did. I can't remember what was talked about, but I remember the thunderous belly-feeling again, a darkness swirling like vomit and bile and shadows and rage, and when it was over I dashed into the bathroom, slamming it locked behind me, and wailed. My hands were on either side of the sink, my shoulders hunched and my head hung low, dripping tears into the mucky plughole. On the way back to the office this time, I rang Gran and told her I was having a bad day, but that I was OK. Hearing her voice was like the first flourishing of spring, and my stomach settled. I picked up a meal deal from Waitrose and I was grateful for my work.

I returned for the third and final time a week later. *Give it a chance*, I told myself, aware that my wry, pretentious cynicism towards the world made me see Badness wherever I looked. I was paranoid about London, about life, and expected the worst on every corner. But I didn't want to snobbishly dismiss the class as childish, even though I already had. I didn't want to think and feel like I was *different* from everyone else and that while whatever was happening here might very well work for them, it certainly wouldn't for me. But I did feel like that. I did, and the knowledge made me ashamed. *Who do you think you are?* I'd ask myself. *I don't know*, I'd answer, *but you* are *a Bad Person*. I don't know what I meant by this, really, but I felt absolutely certain: I was an absence, a hole, a devourer of light. Something was rotten, down to my marrow, and the longer it took to root out, the surer I was that it would spread and eventually I'd crumble to a stinking pile of nothing. By now, it was up to my eyes.

Coming off the antidepressants was less the cliff-drop I expected it to be and more a slow erosion of invisible, unnoticeable contentment (contentment, by nature, doesn't think about itself too often), and I slipped back into the structureless darkness without even realising. I didn't for a second attribute any of my current feelings to the stabilising drug's absence from my blood, and instead put it down to some irreparable fault of my own. A six-week course on 'overcoming worry' felt like a venomous divine joke, and one that I deserved.

Something weird started to happen this time. It can't have been twenty minutes into the talk. Bad thoughts, 'what if' thoughts, were being outlined on the board, and beneath me it felt like the floor was falling away. My head spun dizzy and my hands started to vibrate, slow at first, and then erratic, uncontrollable shuddering seizing every muscle in my body and racking me head to toe. I couldn't breathe, I realised I was crying, gasping for air, shaking all the while, the room silent but for the awkward shuffling of feet on dust-encrusted linoleum. One of the presenters smiled to the other and excused the two of us, and I was shepherded to a side room, into a chair on which I slumped like an old coat, still quivering but the worst behind me. I was a flurry of apologies, for dragging him away, for disrupting the class, *for thinking myself apart from the rest*. Everyone here needed help, who was I to make a scene?

But it really had been unintentional, and now it had passed I felt like I could sleep for a thousand hours. I felt numb, drained, dumbstruck. The shame and guilt would come later. Set alight by the immensity of his concerned gaze, I managed to squeeze the words 'It's more than just worry' out from behind my shuttered teeth. 'I need help.' Usually they wouldn't have passed me on for further care until I'd completed the six-week course, he explained, but he'd refer me to a local charity. Apologies turned to cloying gratitude: 'Thank you thank you thank you,' I proclaimed, regretting the fact I had no laurels or offerings in my work bag to lay at his betrainered feet. Faded bus tickets, years-old lipsticks, stray two-pennies and lint would hardly cut it.

Luckily, the charity – for children and teens up to the age of 25 (I was just-turned 23) – was, again, only around the corner from my work, and one dark winter evening I found myself walking in that direction for a preliminary appointment. It was a small but handsome building located on the cute cobbled street stretching off from the main road on which my office sat – a sudden village beneath a shock of bunting, tiny shops and pubs leading to the river. Inside was warm and smelled homely, and I was eventually led into a tiny room with low chairs and ambient lighting. Once again, I sat across from a smiling face. She was young and beautiful in a plain sort of way, this therapist, and as soon as she spoke I felt the urge to spill my soul onto the round table covered in crayons between us, to thrust myself into her arms and cry into her neck like she was my mam. Her kindness illuminated the room. I shouldn't have been surprised when she said the waiting list was long, but I still felt the crack of her words like a whip. 'Thanks,' I said, and walked to the heaving train station for the long three-train journey back to my not-home. I picked up a kebab from a place in Hammersmith, and when I got home I crawled into my bed, closed the blinds, and let its warm juices spill down my chin.

* * *

There's something unconscionably horrific about receiving emails, isn't there? I don't know if this feeling is specific to people who struggle with anxiety (which, to be fair, would mean everyone) or, well, everyone, but on days when my mind is particularly fractious, receiving any form of notification is nothing short of terrible. They're like Serious Texts, emails – by nature, usually Professional and Of Import. Likely, they will include information I don't like or ask me to do things I don't want to do. Yet most of the time they're couched in work, directed to Work Lauren, which isn't always different to Casual Lauren (as if there were such a person! Everyday Lauren, we'll say, for our purposes here), which means I can with some mental gymnastics hold them at a cognitive arm's length – keep them one step removed from getting to me. They can land in my inbox, but not in my *mind*, or something to that effect. You get me. And you'll understand, then, why getting a call from an unknown number is so bone-chilling.

Unknown numbers bypass the security of Gmail, walk straight into the mind's office, past reception and up the lift, past the receptionist (also Lauren) and straight into Lauren's office faster than I can call security (who are all also Me). Unable to ignore the ringing, vibrating, incessant rectangle in my arse pocket, the shrill clangour slicing the air and interrupting time, I'll pull it out with tremulous hand and upon realising it's not my gran but *an unknown number*, I'll pick up, especially if it's an actual number and not withheld. Withheld tells me it's likely going to be someone ringing about the car accident I didn't have ten years ago, but which my mam did, driven off the road by a huge coach and cut out of the car. I'd be waiting at home, so young, wondering where she is, smelling her pillow and crying.

On the other side of doom there's always glory. And while I resent getting emails as a rule, and indeed unknown-number calls, there's always the possibility that whatever lies on the other side will change my life for the better. That it'll be someone of Great Importance telling me that I Have Been Under-Recognised and Would I Like My Dream Job? I'm not talking about the far-flung relatives who want to transfer $400,000,000 into my bank account TODAY. I'm not stupid. I'm talking about the portals of possibility unopened emails and anonymous calls are. It's like the lottery, but instead of the options being something unimaginably marvellous OR life going on as it is, the choice is between the former OR going to prison for Accidental Tax Evasion or Not Paying My TV Licence. I've always been paranoid to the point of delusional, waiting to be cuffed on the corner for some unknown crime – because, as we've established, I'm a Bad Person. I'll merit the consequences, however medieval. Sometimes I'll leave official-looking letters for weeks at a time, sometimes indefinitely.

And don't get me bloody started on physical letters. Are you trying to give me a fucking heart attack, honestly? Unless of course they're declarations of love or postcards from friends halfway around the world. In which case, yay! Send them my way! Just make sure they quite clearly indicate somewhere – ideally on the envelope – that they're not summonses. These lotteries can be ranked, I guess. Emails are like scratch cards, unknown numbers like the Thunderball, and letters are the mega-rolled-over Euromillions. The ratio of payoff to disappointment escalates depending on the form. With letters, you might well be about to end my life as I know it and snatch away everything I've spent so many years building for myself, but you also might be my best friend sending me handwritten love and there's nothing I love or hold dearer than that.

My gran's an absolute scratch card fiend. Bingo, too. Once, we stood outside the corner shop near hers, next door to the fish and chip shop where we'd bag chippy teas to eat in her little dining room just down the road, as she won scratch card after scratch card. We were so overjoyed we scraped heaven. First a £1 card won another £1 card, the winnings of which purchased another £1 which won £5, and on and on until five or six winning cards must've been purchased. She'd pass us a 2p piece and give us a turn at peeling away the foil, jumping up and down when we saw a little leprechaun emerge, or a pot of gold. In the end we (she) quit while she was ahead, and we were so excited that something so miraculous had happened to *us*. That corner shop was the perfect example of the genre: cardboard boxes mounted against the window with all the crisp types you could ever want: Space Raiders, Monster Munch, that pork crackling that wasn't pork crackling but Pork Crunch, purple Nik Naks (better than sex, them). In front of the till an array of 1p and 2p sweets: fried eggs, squishy shrimps, cola bottles (waste of time), fizzy dummies, chocolate mice, liquorice. In the fridge, 25p bottles of scarily coloured pop, bright red and bright blue. That night we feasted, getting a 50p mixup, crisps *and* pop.

Fifty pence mixups were usually reserved for birthdays. My gran gives *the best* birthday presents. Usually, a scratch card or a pound coin sellotaped inside a birthday card, a carton of our favourite soup (butternut squash from the Big Tesco for me, every time. Liv would get a carton of egg mayonnaise she'd eat out of the tub with a fork [disgusting]), a box of our favourite cereal, or a 50p mixup. I've never looked forward to presents more. The icing on the cake came later, when she'd come round Mam's and make us chopped pork and egg sarnies. But that night we each got a big bag of sweets. My gran doesn't know the meaning of keeping something for herself, by the way. Whatever she has, whether it's £4.70 in coins in her purse or a shock bingo win (this happened once, and I don't know if she kept as much as twenty quid for herself), she'll divvy it out among the family until it's gone. So of course, we – Liv and I, that is – enjoyed the spoils. I was scintillated, absorbed, by the thought that each time we won we were also on the brink of losing it all. Everything! Honestly, it's a wonder my addictive personality and lifelong occupation of only the extreme poles of human emotion have kept me out of casinos.

Maybe if I wasn't so conscientious and, well, me, I'd be a rich tycoon who owned several Vegas hotels by now. I'd rather not think of the alternative. Gran, if you're reading this, you did nothing wrong. I'm a maniac of my own creation and you have done no irreparable damage. I only buy scratch cards now when I need to feel something!

Emails, phone calls and physical letters make me feel this whip-crack of thrilling dread to varying degrees, potential portals all. Behind every curtain there's a disappointing Oz lurking. When that phone call came through then, as I was walking the very short distance between my office in Twickenham and Twickenham Train Station, I let it ring for a moment while I decided what to do. My reflex was to immediately reject the call and to throw my phone over the bridge and under the 17:07 to Wimbledon. But then again it could be a generous benefactor who'd read my articles on IR35 tax legislation and employment tribunals (I worked on an HR magazine) and wanted to make me a writing offer I couldn't refuse, based somewhere on the Amalfi Coast with a beach-side villa included. I had to go back and add 'writing' into that sentence because it was sounding suspiciously like a suspect Sugar Daddy set-up. The potential good outweighed the potential bad on this cheery occasion, and like the heroine in a horror movie sans knife grabbed hastily from the kitchen, I picked up with a quiet 'Hello?'

My bet paid off. I wasn't going to jail! I was flooded with emotion. I had a whole life ahead of me! And, apparently, an eight-week course of charity-funded counselling a mere one-minute walk away from my office starting next week. I couldn't believe my luck and profusely thanked and thanked and thanked the receptionist as though I'd just won an Oscar or been told a heart transplant match had been found or the production team at *Long Lost Family* had found a long-lost brother. God knows what the other people waiting for the next train to Richmond thought, but in that moment I didn't care.

It was during these sessions with the smiley, warm counsellor that my picking accidentally came up. Like I said before, I wasn't even thinking about telling her because I didn't at that time see it as a problem. I'd not articulated it to myself, didn't have the vocabulary or understanding yet to call it what it was, but as I sat across from her in the ambiently lit room on a chair too low to be comfortable (I had to kind of fall into it like a sack of spuds, and it took a great effort of strength and will to get out of it again. Maybe it was a metaphor) she said, 'I've noticed you keep touching your face.'

Well, I hadn't. But it seems I was trying to unconsciously sooth myself while I articulated my darkness, and she'd spotted it. 'Let's try and not do it until the end of the session, see if you can.' I succeeded, because then I was just a social smoker when it came to picking. I did it as and when, and OK, I'd just been doing it without realising, but I wasn't on twenty a day yet. As the sessions rolled on, though, I was annoyingly becoming more aware of it. I'd catch myself running my hand over my face as we spoke, and then at work and then on the train to work, and then before I knew it my day was consumed with whether or not I was touching my face. Trying not to made me want to do it more. At the end of a particularly gruelling counselling session, from which I got a £20+ Uber home because I was just emptied, I asked if I could stay just for five minutes because I knew the second I left her room I'd dash to the toilet down the way to pick furiously at my face in the tiny speckled mirror above the loo. It was only my face then, by the way. The fire was a new-kindled flame at this point, but it was getting hotter.

Soon we moved on to other things and didn't mention the picking again. After every session, I'd put the lid down on that toilet, kneel on it with one leg and have a go at my face for ten minutes, or however long it took me to calm down. The sessions came to an end – I'd had them extended because I was scared, but in the end didn't need extra because I was done for now. It hadn't focused on my current issues really, more the past.

We addressed, briefly, how I was numbing myself with content. I couldn't even put the bins out without listening to a podcast. As soon as I woke up, I had one in my ears, probably about some horrific murder, and I'd only take it out the second I stepped into the office. As soon as I left I'd have it in again, and when I got home I'd binge Netflix. I was also addicted to Candy Crush so would play that to drown the world out, too. My therapist challenged me to do nothing on my journey to work as often as I could. To just be on the tube, looking out the window, *thinking. Being.*

I tried one day. As the tube ascended out of Hammersmith Station's gloom and into bright morning sunshine, I felt good. I enjoyed watching the people get on and off the tube, exchanged smiles with some of the regulars I saw every day, and appreciated the differently roofed houses as they dashed by. But with every stop we went through I slipped. I couldn't stop thinking about what I was doing, my inner narrator going mad. *I'm on a tube and I am trying to be in the moment. I'm on a tube and I am trying to be in the moment. I'm sitting here with my thoughts. So what should I think about?* All I could think about was the fact I was on the tube trying to be in the moment. I felt claustrophobic again, my breath shortening, and I couldn't take it any longer. I put my headphones back in and told her that yeah, I'd definitely noticed a difference.

My fears that my therapy hadn't worked were assuaged when, a couple of weeks after, some friends and I took the train from Paddington out into the countryside to the hen do of one of my best friends. The house, which was more of a wisteria-kissed cottage, stood miles apart from other dwellings and overlooked rolling green fields. The garden was massive and felt even huger being surrounded so openly with yet more wide, green space. We played hide-and-seek in it and, at night, sat on hay bales around a crackling fire all snuggled under blankets. At the end of the couple of days, I realised, like a splash to the face, that

I had successfully lost myself. I'd left my inner narrator in London, hadn't heard Simon once.

On the train back to London I got quieter and quieter, retreating into myself. I was with my friends Natalie and Eleanor, and we had to sit in the footwell near the doors because it was absolutely rammed. About half an hour away from home I unexpectedly burst into tears. We were already sat as close as possible to one another, squeezed as we were hip to hip, but they managed to get closer and cuddle me. 'I … don't want to live in London any more,' I wept. 'I'm so unhappy.' I'd said to my therapist that I was struggling in the city, that I'd felt like I was on a bad holiday and staying in a shit Travelodge waiting in my heart to just go home. I'd said as much to Dad too when he visited, breaking down in Soho after we couldn't find anywhere with space enough for a pint. Anyway, my therapist gently told me to consider my options. 'You've only got yourself to answer to,' she said. I didn't realise until that moment on the train how my every muscle had absorbed those life-altering words, had soaked them in like rain-drenched trees after a drought. 'You don't have to live here,' my friends said, and for the first time I felt it to be true. Having left them at Paddington to go our own ways, standing on the cold tube platform I rang my boyfriend in Cambridge. 'Can I come live with you in Cambridge?' I asked. I wasn't scared of his answer because I knew what it would be, what it would always be. 'Of course you can, my love.' Within a month, I'd left. He and I would live in his single-bed university room before moving into a flat of our own. My spirits soared and I could feel myself returning to me through the haze, ready to reattach. I welcomed her with open arms.

The issue of picking only came up again a couple of months later at my new job. I had a word for it by now, having Googled 'skin picking can't stop' while I was still in London, during my therapy. I still didn't think it was a problem, though, or at least not one that I couldn't just stop when I wanted to. I wasn't going to test that hypothesis, of course, because I wanted to continue, so I lived in denial for a bit. By the time I started my new job at a local newspaper, I'd started picking at my chest, as well as my face. But I just ignored it. So what if it calmed me down? I was living at a difficult time, I thought to myself, having just made a big life decision and moving away and trying to sort a proper flat for me and Jovan so we didn't have to sleep in a single bed together. New job, too, and that was always stressful. So I let it slide. My therapist had told me, in another of her morsels of wisdom I'd collected like shells on a beach, to let myself off the hook. I was abusing this particular lesson, using it to feed my denial and fuel my compulsion, my addiction.

It was during a one-to-one meeting with one of the reporters I was managing at the time that it hit me like a ton of bricks. We'd been going through an article she'd written, line for line, when all of a sudden she apologetically said, 'Oh gosh, sorry, you're bleeding.' I reached up to my face, knowing it was coming from there, and my finger came back red. I'd been unconsciously fussing a spot at my desk all morning, I realised, and now my face was bleeding. I was mortified. I hastily excused myself. Locking the bathroom door behind me, I wound and wound more tissue paper than I needed around my fist like a bandage and sat on the toilet, letting streams of tears flow down my cheeks. I tilted my head back so it wouldn't leave white rivulets in my thick make-up (even when I had to get fuller and fuller coverage foundations, I ignored the fact, and instead slapped it over the problem, concealed it), using my makeshift boxing glove to dab at spots of blood and tears alike. I went back into the meeting room quickly and with a 'sorry about that' got back to it. I kept my head down and my eyes averted the whole time.

When I got home, I rifled through the notes on my iPhone, trying to find the name of the psychological service my Cambridge GP had recommended. I should've mentioned that when I got back to Cambridge I realised I absolutely should not have come off my medication. It seemed so obvious, so stupid. I'd stopped because I'd felt better, which is the ironic reason lots of people stop taking antidepressants. It hadn't occurred to me that I was feeling better at least in part because of them. So, I'd started taking them again, and after the initial few weeks of nausea and headaches had worn off, they were stabilising me again. I was getting up early to go to work, was regularly showering and exercising, getting on with the quiet business of living. Occupying the middle ground: not ecstatic, not miserable, but content.

Apart from the picking.

I took the call with the service in the same office where my face had bled. I'd tried to move it outside of working hours, but they couldn't, and I was desperate. After a pleasant conversation explaining, shyly, what I'd been doing and, panicking, how it was spreading, I answered a few questions that ultimately determined I needed 'High Intensity Cognitive Behavioural Therapy' urgently. Unexpectedly I felt relief. I *did* have a problem and wasn't wrong in seeking help. I wouldn't have been wrong what-ever the case, but in that moment I was overcome. Tears of joy turned to tears of helplessness pretty quickly as they told me I'd have to wait between nine and ten months to access the therapy I apparently urgently needed. 'You just said urgently,' I said to the woman, in whose voice I could read the hundreds of identical conversations she'd had. Her apology was dressed in frustration as she calmly but firmly explained to me that services were tight and waiting lists long. I loved her, I hated her, I wanted to scream at her, I wanted to beg her, I did beg her. I slipped again into numbness, shutting down, entering autopilot and letting myself drift away somewhere deep and untouchable while I dealt with the paperwork of being. Monotonously I answered 'yes' when she asked whether I wanted to be put on the waiting list before hanging up without saying 'bye'. I deflated in my chair, suddenly bone-tired and incapable of walking out of this room and over to my desk.

After an indeterminate amount of time with my head in my arms on the table, staring at it blankly, I somehow managed. Tears were welling in my eyes not long after. I couldn't see anything on the screen, didn't want to, and I let it blur into a white wobbly blob. I asked Anna, the manager who sat right behind me, with her back to me, for a chat, please? We entered yet another meeting room and I said I needed to go home. Intuitive and lovely, she knew I had to and didn't ask any questions. The office was located, frustratingly, at Cambridge Research Park. I say frustratingly, because it wasn't in Cambridge, but off a main road in the middle of nowhere. The bus stop serving the complex was right outside our office, which sat just off the roundabout turnoff, but buses only came once an hour through the day. So I sat outside in my big fluffy bear coat and put a podcast about murder in my ears. The bus eventually came and took me home to bed.

Winter turned to spring, and I would spend my half-hour lunch walking the fields behind the industrial park in the cold sunshine. I'd come back to the office with muddy boots. In March 2020, like the rest of the world, we stopped coming into the office and instead worked from home. An email came mid-August offering me my first CBT appointment, and so the Zoom calls every Wednesday morning began. I was by that time already going through the redundancy process, on the precipice of the frightful unknown again. Now it's November, and robins are starting to sing outside my window, perched on the roofs across the way. My therapy has finished, now, and while it's given me strategies to try and cope, still – disappointingly – my relentless picking persists.

9
Parrot

Over the years, I've come to really identify with my gran's bald, grey parrot. Or rather, former parrot – not that it's transformed or anything, though I realise that's what that sounds like – but we'll get on to that.

I identify with him because he was at once a hilarious legend and a neurotic nightmare. He was called Coco and he maniacally pulled his feathers out until his pink wrinkled skin was exposed, prompting one's gorge to rise ever so slightly in that particular *hmm, no, that's not right, that* mode usually reserved for ghastly Siamese cats that resemble baby Voldemort tumbling out of the cloth and into the cauldron in Harry Potter 4 (if you know, you know).

My grandma's house smells like warm cooking oil, freshly washed clothes and instant coffee. In the living room, which you reach almost as soon as you enter the house, you'll find my grandad – likened often and by all to Super Mario on account of his frankly voluptuous tash – in his big black cracked-leather armchair watching one black-and-white Western classic after another, while grazing on food prepared by my gran. He's getting on now, so the volume is on *loud*. Beside him is an old electric radiator, the kind that glows in warm orange lines behind a protective metal grate and clinks on with an initial hum and rattle, and a dusty bookshelf full of Roy Chubby Brown DVDs. Walk through there and you'll get to the dining room, where my grandma sits in the corner (in a chair, not having succumbed yet to knee-clasped rocking back and forth) trying not to go insane as innumerable shootouts take place next door and rattle the very foundations of the house. She escapes into her crosswords and drinks lots of tea.

Don't worry if my grandad doesn't say hello when you walk through, by the way; most any of us get is a low grunt of acknowledgement. No, the most words he strings together are ones asking my gran to perform tasks for him, usually food related. Liv and I were round visiting once, in the dining room at the kitchen table of course, when he shouted through the door, 'Mary, I want an egg.' When she said, 'We don't have any eggs,' he just repeated: 'I want. An egg.' She's spunky and gives it back as much as she gets, doing it all with a good-humoured laugh, but he pushes his luck. It's not unusual for me to be on the phone with her only for his voice to boom in the background, 'There's not enough rice with this, Mare.' Short for Mary, of course, but we all know who the real effing 'mare is.

Anyway, through the dining room you'll get to the kitchen – my grandma's territory. Nothing much to note here other than that the fridge is, as surely all grandmas' fridges are, adorned with various magnets, photos, and kids' artwork. Out in the mostly concrete, small back garden, there used to be two sheds filled floor to ceiling with caged birds. Budgies, probably, but I think there were different types. Sometimes we'd be allowed to peek in as kids, and I remember it smelled musty and thinking how gloomy and sad it seemed. Also, all that screeching was not for me. My grandad's appreciation for birds, if you could call caging them appreciation, was probably behind his decision to get a grey parrot with a shot of bright red through a tail he couldn't have possibly known would end up being the highlight of a kind of ugly self-styled mullet.

The parrot's tall metal cage was situated in the dining room with my gran, who upon his arrival suddenly had not only the Westerns to drown out but the frequent chattering of a loquacious bird who, in perfectly articulated Teesside tones, repeated things she and my grandad said. He perched on a swinging wooden block and bit at the bars, talons at angles clutching and climbing them, whether to escape or simply get more attention we don't know. The twang would echo every time his beak hit the metal and you could see his barbaric little black tongue darting this way and that. When Liv and I visited he'd repeat such classics as 'CaniyavacuppateaMary?', 'Cuppa? Cuppa tea?', 'Yalright pet' (My gran's preferred phone greeting) and 'Love ya, bye.' Whatever else lay in the cheeky lad's comprehensive though unoriginal repertoire, beyond a single piercing shriek of varying lengths, is sadly lost to the sands of time.

Coco clattered and clanged and struck the unfortunate bell that presumably came as built-in amusement – surely designed, like the squeak in dog toys, by a scorned pet in an evil lair with a cackling vendetta against all human adults. Like the telly blaring next door, and the old man slowly becoming one with a chair, he was loud and proud. When he was intermittently given the attention he clearly so desperately craved, which is to say when Liv or I would go right up to the cage and look him in the eye, he'd cock his head to one side so as to direct one beady, white-rimmed eye at you like an old hooded crone you've encountered in the woods who says 'Well, well, well, what have we got here?' while peering at you out of her one good eye under the glow of a lamp she's holding aloft.

Just about the only time he wasn't being a nuisance to everyone around him, much like myself, was when he was biting and plucking and picking himself. His feathers lay scattered, grey and white, among his droppings at the bottom of his cage. I suppose in psychiatric terms you could say he was suffering from trichotillomania, but even once the feathers were gone he'd tease and torment his wrinkly skin as though there was more to pluck, which better resembles dermatillomania. In fact, in the bird world, it's got a name of its own: pterotillomania (feather picking). Like, can your heart even friggin' deal? Wikipedia says it's a maladaptive behavioural disorder 'commonly seen in captive birds which chew, bite or pluck their own feathers with their beak, resulting in damage to the feathers and occasionally the skin'. And beyond the close resemblance to human behavioural equivalents, hair pulling has also been reported in mice, guinea pigs, rabbits, sheep and muskox, dogs and cats. It can be caused by too boring an environment (making it more complex can help, apparently) and loneliness. I particularly love this Wikipedia writer's tragicomic streak, which slightly stops the whole thing from being a completely devastating read. They write: 'These birds may not deal well with a solitary lifestyle.' No shit.

In the process of writing this, I asked my gran where he went, since I couldn't remember whether he'd died or what – one day he just wasn't there – and she casually told me they'd had to give him to one of my grandad's friends who also had parrots because she contracted a life-threatening disease from either him or the companion they eventually got for him – Smoky, quieter, with a more menacing vibe – that nearly killed her. Apparently, nobody in the family knew this because she didn't want to worry anyone, but *Jesus bloody Christ, woman*. I know I said I identified with him and how toxic he was to those who surrounded him, but Jesus. Also, I hope my grandad's parrot-loving friend didn't contract the disease too. Seems a bit harsh to be honest, but surely he appreciated, as the old saying goes, that there's no such thing as a free parrot.

Anyhow, under the shadow of him doing this to himself, as kids, Liv and I would play on the floor of the dining room with a plastic kitchenette replete with twisty knobs and opening doors, and a shopping trolley filled with plastic groceries, like those bits of bread with squares of

Velcro on their bellies that made a sandwich when you slapped them together (how bloody satisfying were these things? Like somehow better than the actual versions of what they represented? Tin of beans: No. Fake tin of beans made out of plastic: YES, a thousand times yes). Gran would make us sandwiches – real ones – and get us drinks out of the little minifridge in the corner and we'd add to the incessant cacophony of noise doing her head in by sticking together and unsticking wooden slices of Velcroed pizza. I wonder now whether toys, like the bell, helped Coco.

If I'm honest, I'm sceptical they made any difference. One of the main strategies for coping with skin picking, I learnt on the internet and also during CBT, is rerouting the energy into something else, like a fiddle toy. Fiddle toys are little bits of plastic or sometimes metal that range from fidget spinners, plastic peas popping out of a plastic pod, stress balls that push contained goo through holes (which to be fair is very satisfying) to metal spinny puzzle things. I hate puzzles, so the latter is a big no-no for me. My boyfriend once bought me a wooden puzzle toy as a gift and I burst into tears because I didn't like puzzles and God bless him, he wasn't to know. So no puzzles, but squeezy things that have the potential to pop? Now we're cooking.

But herein lies the problem. The only satisfaction I get out of them is the possibility of destruction, which doesn't really lend itself well to objects. True to my roots as an institutionalised success-obsessed attention seeker, there has, for me, to be an *end point*. I know puzzles have one, usually, but it takes effort rather than brute force to get there, which is my modus operandi. No, they need a dramatic, orgasmic, fireworky end point. A happy ending, if you will. To my former therapist, who I know is probably reading this, I know that this end point *should* be my calmness and contentedness. And that is my goal, it really is, but there's just no showbiz to being at one with yourself. Such serenity requires patience and an absence of action and movement over time, and is easily eclipsed by the perennial heart- and belly-tug of an irresistible impulse that promises (yet always fails to deliver, long term) release *right now*. Like any addiction, its trick is to give you the hit you crave before draining you completely of relief and feel-good juices, leaving behind only shame and renewed restlessness, trapping you in its insidious cycle of euphoric highs and heart-breaking lows.

Just as I thwarted my mam's attempt to stop me biting my nails when I was in primary school by finding a way to circumvent the intended response, so I unintentionally co-opted fiddle toys. After a session of CBT in which we decided to give these hand-distracters a go, I went out and bought a bright pink squishy ball filled up with some kind of foam that tantalisingly rose to the translucent surface like a secret. It was a thing of beauty, let me tell you. Plunging my hands into it felt like kneading forbidden bread and it was great fun to chuck. Me and Jovan would fling it back and forth across our living room at mounting speeds and bounce it mercilessly off one another's unsuspecting bonces. I grew quite attached to it and despite all my worst instincts managed to resist the urge to fucking obliterate it.

That is, until I noticed a weak spot. It couldn't, after all, be a perfect sphere. How the hell would they have got all that sweet, sweet foamy stuff inside? There was a circle of thicker plastic at the bottom, or top I suppose, and the more I played with the ball the more it seemed to fray and stretch. I was squeezing it while watching telly one night when I felt a ridge where once there had been only smoothness. A surge of familiar anticipation swelled in me and I did something I'm still proud of: I put it down. I knew I couldn't resist, so I did.

But sadly, the seed was already planted and the toy was tainted from there on out. I still played with it, but it was marred. Instead of being the mindless thing I needed, I suddenly had to be very mindful when playing with it, which was the exact opposite of what I wanted. I wanted to escape thinking, not do more of it. A few days later we went for a walk along the river with a visiting friend with whom we'd got royally smashed the night before, and I tucked the ball beneath a blanket stuffed at the bottom of the tote bag we took with us. We spread it out on a river-bank half an hour or so into our walk, and lazed beneath the waning summer sun. Alcohol always makes my jitter-iness worse (oh how I miss the days when hangovers just meant vomiting, and not crushing existential dread coupled with the conviction none of your friends actually like you), so almost as soon as we sat down I pulled out the ball and squeezed. I'm not ashamed to say I first wrote 'squoze' there, which the past tense of 'squeeze' should absolutely be. My mind was a tangled mess of half-thoughts written by my fingers on the ball, and as soon as I rediscovered that ridge it was all over. The weak point didn't need much coaxing at all and eventually – ah – a tiny split appeared. Unable to hold on any longer, I squoze as hard as I could and the white foam came forcefully pouring out. What was contained had been released, the world was set aright. But … it wasn't.

The sagging, soggy sack lay limp in my hands, which were now uncomfortably sticky. My friend and boyfriend noticed and laughed with a 'What the hell?' And I too laughed it off. Don't get me wrong, it had felt absolutely amazing, but only for an infinitesimal beat of time. Then it felt really, really bad. I was awash with shame; it thundered through me, and I felt completely out of control, like I was falling and would be falling forever and that the only thing to snap me back would be to do it again and again and again until I was irrevocably lost – no Lauren, just a cycle of pain and release until I died. My head felt fizzy, like I'd stood up too fast and all the blood had rushed to it. I faux-nonchalantly stuffed the unrecognisable deflated thing into a plastic tub, which until moments ago had housed Sainsbury's houmous, and had to carry it until we reached a bin, somewhere back towards home.

Playing with and ultimately destroying the pink ball thankfully taught me something invaluable: there doesn't need to be an end point. I was shocked and, for a couple of weeks, utterly destroyed by the fact I had finished a course of High Intensity Cognitive Behavioural Therapy without actually stopping the behaviour. I'd gone through several stress balls and fiddle toys that simply couldn't withstand the brutal insatiability of my hands. When I destroyed that big pink one, the high was almost immediately replaced by a genuine sadness that I wouldn't have it in my flat with me any more, and the sadness lasted longer. Much longer.

The high, I realised, was a lie. I know it's a lie. I know it fails to live up to its promise, that it isn't an end point in itself. That in life, if I'm lucky, there'll always be an *afterwards*. After all, despite what my anxiety tells me, I'm not frozen, paralysed, in time. Moments follow moments follow moments, and if I'm going to endure, I'm going to have to find a way of getting through them without feeling trapped in time, like white foam in a pink ball, desperately claustrophobic and dying to break free.

Continuity is what I'm going for, these days. Longevity. It isn't easy. I still have a box of fiddle toys, but I rarely play with them because I'm too worried I'll fall prey to the vicious possibility fizzing at the heart of every one of them, of me. When I do, it's only for short bursts, but I'm good now at putting them away when I'm tempted to tear into them. Some are only partially rather than fully broken. I've not had the same luck with my skin, unfortunately.

Some things have genuinely helped me stop picking, if not forever then at least for some time, which I'll list here:

- **Showering in the dark:** Now, as you can imagine this isn't something for the fainthearted. In fact, for legal reasons I urge you not to try this at home and assume zero liability if you do. OK, I'm being dramatic, but I have slipped and seen my life flash before my eyes a few times. Miraculously, I've never ended up actually body slamming the bathtub, but even just the feeling of my heart leaping to my throat in the long seconds before I somehow managed to right myself is enough to make this one of my least favourite strategies. It turns out I don't *need* to see my skin breaking – my fingertips are like police dogs able to sniff out even the tiniest of bumps – but I don't get half the satisfaction without sight. So being in the dark worked, just not in the shower. For that reason, I'll give this method 7/10.

- **Bathing in the dark:** The bath has always been my happy place. For as long as I can remember, I've read my book in the bath until the water is cold and my toes shrivelled, so the way picking started to ruin it was one of the reasons I sought help. I say ruin because the bathroom is my trigger, which is to say it's the place I'm most likely to self-destruct. Instead of a sanctuary it became deeply distressing, because I couldn't be trusted not to tear my chest to shreds. It would only take one little bump to set me off, and only when the trance-like state I'd fallen into passed would I realise I was covered in blood. So, I got a clip-on portable reading light that allowed me to have the bathroom light off while still being able to read in the bath. This worked wonders as I tore my way through *The Thursday Murder Club* and I thought I'd really cracked it, but alas it's only really good for hardback books. I found that when I clipped it onto the cover of a paperback, the adjustable arm wobbled and swung with every movement and turned page, like the barbaric swoops of an aggravated goose's long neck. The resultant light show was enough to give me a headache and I had to give up and turn the light on. Plus, it made the book way more unsteady in my hands and I've already lost more than one book to the depths by accidentally dropping it in without the added help of a sentient reading light. Particularly devastating was the loss of Charles Dickens' chunky *David Copperfield*, which slammed into the water hard and was entirely submerged before I could save it. It eventually dried out but has never been the same since. For this reason, the bathing in the dark technique gets 6/10.

NOTE: *Any light shed on my skin was a trigger to pick, so another iteration of this was the discovery that the switch to turn off the bathroom's light entirely was located above the door frame and therefore out of my reach. Jovan would turn it off every evening – dusk falling being another trigger for me – and it worked until I realised if I did a little jump I could surreptitiously turn it on again. The moral of the story: believe in yourself and you'll reach heights you could never have imagined.*

- **Bathing chaperoned:** When I was little and went in the bath, Liv would sometimes come into the bathroom and sit on the toilet seat to keep me company and chat with me while I soaked. Now, my poor boyfriend has been roped into doing the same thing, sitting in the bathroom with me while I bathe in order to gently say the word 'hands' whenever he hears a flick of water that might suggest inappropriate hand movement or sees me scanning my face. It makes me love and hate him so much. I loathe this method because it works. But, of course, my boyfriend can't be my 24-hour carer, I wouldn't want him to be, and my little enemy knows he'll help, so sometimes I purposefully don't ask him to do this because I want to pick and don't want him interrupting me. It's complicated, OK? A begrudged 9/10.

- **Wearing plasters on my fingertips:** This helps for the five minutes I'm able to keep them on before tearing them off. Turns out it's hard to get anything done thus impeded. Also, it feels good and naughty to rip them off when I know I shouldn't. *Haha, fuck you for trying to help yourself, Lauren,* Lauren says to Lauren. *Think you can get past me? I mean, you?* 5/10. Very confusing.

NOTE: *Wearing plasters on my chest – though not face – does help, when I can keep them on.*

- **Clay masks:** By this I mean a clay mask slopped onto my face and chest in great big handfuls, or fancy bath stuff. Let's tackle the former, first. This is a good method because if I touch covered areas while the mask is still wet, I just get the gloopy crap all over my hands, which then transfers to the pages of my book. So far so good. But washing it all off before getting out of the bath requires more attention to the areas I pick than would otherwise be the case, thereby defeating the purpose of the whole activity entirely. Also, being a tight arse means I refuse to spend real money on these masks, so they actually cause more spots to appear. 2/10 (They smell nice, I guess?).

- **Fancy baths:** Ensuring the experience is as akin to a relaxing spa trip as possible can and does make it more enjoyable, and I feel focused on the soothing, self-caring aspect of the bath if I zhuzh it up a bit. Not too much though. One especially involved bath bomb that released leaves and petals did make me feel momentarily like that famous painting of Ophelia in the pond, though not ... dead, just beautiful and ethereal; however, upon getting out of the bath, wet foliage was plastered to my body and I looked like a swamp creature emerging from the boggy depths. Also, sometimes this method just doesn't work and I pick anyway. Probably a state of mind thing. 10/10 for fun. 5–7/10 for helping picking.

None of these things have stopped my picking entirely. I wanted there to be a grand, triumphant ending to this story of frenetic impulses and heart-stopping moments, but I realise now that life should for the most part be adoringly, wondrously dull, and I intend to end my story that way. I want to be bored out of my skull and know that I'm still living my best life, despite the upward trajectory branded on us from childhood. I've always wanted so hard to be inarguably *excellent*, at the top of my profession, any profession, the skinniest and most beautiful and richest, where I finally didn't have to run any more. But there isn't a top, is there? There'll always be an afterwards; none of these things can shield you from the sometimes painful reality of being alive.

I think this – the *afterwards* – is true of selves, too. Although CBT hasn't, alas, stopped my picking, it has opened a window out of which I can see that there's a future where I don't do it. It just doesn't feel inevitable any more, which for someone whose claustrophobia extends from sitting in the middle row of a theatre, or being stuck on a bus without a loo, to feeling trapped in time, is nothing short of miraculous.

With this final revelation, though, comes a caveat it would be dishonest of me not to mention. As the number of sessions I had left wound down from three to two to one, my panic rising that I was still picking and why hadn't it *worked*, this glimmer of hope for a picking-free future was clouded by a developing fear gathering, like a storm, apace.

Tipping glasses over turned into worrying I was going to be struck down by Almighty God for lying, then to weeing a bajillion times a day, to biting my nails until they bled, to picking my skin. What had felt like the most random thing in the world for me to start doing was suddenly exposed to be just another breadcrumb on a very long trail that began in a small Billingham cul-de-sac. The signs had been there all along, and while it was reassuring that each phase ended, I was terrified to discover that the recession of one epoch simply gave rise to another one entirely. Moment after moment after moment. Would picking be just another crumb? Sure, I was ecstatic to finally be able to envision a future in which I didn't do the hideous thing I'd been doing for what felt like forever, the thing that felt like an inevitability, but what was going to come next? It was like the same chaotic energy had been shapeshifting over the years and would never go away.

But I've been shapeshifting too. This Lauren is dead set that this will be the end of the road. *I'm stronger than it*, I tell myself, *and I'm in control*. I can't see another road forking off this one yet, but if one doesn't appear any time soon, I'm quite content to rip a trail through the woods. I don't need to see it from above. And hey, until now I hadn't been able to see the road at all. I'm learning to palm read, in my own way, and I don't think disruptions to the lifeline are necessarily the foreboding signs Mam's books once said they were.

As I sit and write now, I feel all the past Laurens nearby, as if they're all sitting around me in my living room that's blinking with candlelight. Beside me on the sofa is very little me, wild curly hair tumbling down her back, holding my index finger tightly while looking around the room we can call ours in awe (as well as scanning for the nearest exits and likely route to the toilet). On the floor awkwardly sexting her boyfriend is teenage me, her head a mop of bright red, over-hairsprayed curls shaved at the sides, without a clue about who she is and unable to envision herself beyond the age of 22, max. She's probably thinking *I could do with having my eyebrows waxed*, even though there are barely any left after her over-zealous plucking. There's hair-extensioned me and fake-tanned me and skinny me and fat me, in love me and heartbroken me, goth-phase me and another me who's just left the room under the guise of needing the toilet to put her fingers down her throat until she gags, because some inner voice won't let her relax until she does.

All the Livs are here too. I can't claim to know what they're thinking beyond being, at times, justifiably sick of the many Laurens' shit, but I feel aglow in the heart-knowledge that whichever Lauren walks through the door next, a Liv I've not yet met is also on her way.

Acknowledgements

Before I start thanking those of you who've supported me – not just while I wrote this book but as friends, at whatever stage of my life – an apology to those I'll inevitably, accidentally, miss out.

Firstly, thank you to my endlessly patient, kind and thoughtful editor (/therapist), Jon, without whom this book simply would not be what it is today. Thanks for believing in it and me. You and all the wonderful HarperNorth team are legends – I'll always, always appreciate everything.

I'd also like to thank my partner, Jovan, who I love more than words; my sister Liv, who is everything to me; and all my family and friends, in particular my dearest friend Callum, my university friends and all the girls from home. You all keep me going, smiling, trying.

Special thanks go to my agent Marilia, who has been just a beacon of light for as long as we've worked together; long may it continue.

Thanks, too, to Claudia Canavan, who commissioned my first ever writing on the topic of skin picking; to the wonderful mother of my great friend Charlotte, Rachel

Grace, who looked after me while I was struggling with picking in Cambridge; to Paula Wain and Fiona Lodge, former English teachers who helped me believe in myself; to Ross Wilson and Robert Macfarlane for the same, and for helping me find myself during some of the most difficult and glorious years of my life.

I'd also like to give a shout-out to the Picking Me Foundation, the only donor-supported non-profit worldwide focused on Dermatillomania – if you're struggling, I would really recommend checking them out.

Harper
North

Book Credits

HarperNorth would like to thank the following staff
and contributors for their involvement in making
this book a reality:

Hannah Avery	Jean-Marie Kelly
Fionnuala Barrett	Oliver Malcolm
Claire Boal	Simon Moore
Charlotte Brown	Anna Morrison
Sarah Burke	Alice Murphy-Pyle
Alan Cracknell	Adam Murray
Jonathan de Peyer	Melissa Okusanya
Anna Derkacz	Genevieve Pegg
Tom Dunstan	Agnes Rigou
Kate Elton	James Ryan
Mick Fawcett	Florence Shepherd
Simon Gerratt	Angela Snowden
Monica Green	Hannah Stamp
Graham Holmes	Emma Sullivan
Megan Jones	Katrina Troy

For more unmissable reads,
sign up to the HarperNorth newsletter at
www.harpernorth.co.uk

or find us on Twitter at
@HarperNorthUK

Harper
North